# BILOXI
# BLUES

# BILOXI
# BLUES

## NEIL SIMON

RANDOM HOUSE 🏠 NEW YORK

Library of Congress Cataloging-in-Publication Data
Simon, Neil.
Biloxi blues.
I. Title.
PS3537.I663B55   1986      812'.54      85-24173
ISBN 0-394-55139-7

Manufactured in the United States of America
9 8 7 6 5 4 3 2
First Edition

For my grandson Andrew Leland

BILOXI BLUES *was first presented on December 8, 1984, at the Ahmanson Theatre, Los Angeles, and on March 28, 1985, at the Neil Simon Theatre, New York City, with the following cast:*

| | |
|---|---|
| ROY SELRIDGE | Brian Tarantina |
| JOSEPH WYKOWSKI | Matt Mulhern |
| DON CARNEY | Alan Ruck |
| Eugene Morris Jerome | Matthew Broderick |
| ARNOLD EPSTEIN | Barry Miller |
| Sgt. MERWIN J. TOOMEY | Bill Sadler |
| JAMES HENNESEY | Geoffrey Sharp |
| ROWENA | Randall Edwards |
| DAISY HANNIGAN | Penelope Ann Miller |

*Directed by* Gene Saks
*Setting by* David Mitchell
*Lighting by* Tharon Musser
*Costumes by* Ann Roth

# SYNOPSIS OF SCENES

## ACT ONE

## ACT TWO

The action takes place in Biloxi and Gulfport, Mississippi, in 1943.

# ACT ONE

*The coach of an old railroad train, pressed into service because of the war.*

*It is 1943.*

*(All set pieces are representational, stylized and free-flowing. We have a lot of territory to cover here . . .)*

*Four soldiers, dressed in fatigues, from eighteen to twenty years old, are stretched out across the coach seats, facing each other, their legs reaching out onto the opposite seats. Three of the soldiers are sleeping. They are* JOSEPH WYKOWSKI, ROY SELRIDGE *and* DON CARNEY. *The fourth boy is* EUGENE MORRIS JEROME. *He is awake and sitting up, writing in a school notebook. It is quiet except for the rumbling of the train along the tracks. A fifth boy,* ARNOLD EPSTEIN, *sleeps in the baggage rack above the others.*

*It is night and a single light illuminates the group.* ROY, *in an effort to get more comfortable, turns and his shoeless foot crawls practically into* WYKOWSKI'S *mouth.* WYKOWSKI, *annoyed, slaps* ROY'S *foot away.*

SELRIDGE *(Waking)* Hey! What the hell's with you?

WYKOWSKI Get your foot out of my mouth, horse-face.

SELRIDGE Up your keester with a meathook, Kowski.

CARNEY Knock it off, pissheads.

WYKOWSKI Go take a flying dump, Carney.

CARNEY Yeah. In your mother's hairnet, homo!
  *(They all return to sleeping)*

EUGENE *(Aloud to the audience)* . . . It was my fourth day in the army and so far I hated everyone . . . We were on a filthy train riding from Fort Dix, New Jersey, to Biloxi, Mississippi, and in three days nobody washed. The aroma was murder. We were

3

supposed to be fighting Germany and Japan but instead we were stinking up America.

(*The train rumbles along . . .* ROY *peers out the window*)

SELRIDGE  Where the hell are we? (EUGENE *is still engrossed in his writing.* ROY *kicks him*) Hey! Shakespeare! Where the hell are we?

EUGENE  West Virginia.

SELRIDGE  No shit? . . . Where's that near?

EUGENE  You don't know where West Virginia is? Didn't you ever take Geography?

SELRIDGE  I was sick that day.

EUGENE  You don't know what part of the country it's in?

SELRIDGE  (*Rises and grabs his crotch*)  Yeah. *This* part. Up yours, Jerome.

EUGENE  (*Reads what he has written*)  "Roy Selridge from Schenectady, New York, smelled like a tuna-fish sandwich left out in the rain. He thought he had a terrific sense of humor but it was hard to laugh at a guy who had cavities in nineteen out of thirty-two teeth."

(*The train rumbles on*)

WYKOWSKI (*Opens his eyes*)  Jesus Christ! Who did that?

EUGENE  What?

WYKOWSKI  Someone let one go! . . . Holy Jeez. (*He fans his cap in front of his face*) I need a gas mask . . . (*He lights a match*) You writing all this stuff in your diary? "Major fart in West Virginia."

EUGENE  It's not a diary. It's my memoirs.

4

WYKOWSKI  Well, you don't have to write it down because *that* one will stay in your book forever . . . Whoo! Jeez!
*(He goes back to sleep)*

EUGENE *(To the audience)*  Joseph Wykowski from Bridgeport, Connecticut, had two interesting characteristics. He had the stomach of a goat and could eat anything. His favorite was Hershey bars with the wrappers still on it . . . The other peculiar trait was that he had a permanent erection. I'm talking about night and day, during marching or sleeping. There's no explaining this phenomenon unless he has a unique form of paralysis.
*(The train rumbles on in the night)*

CARNEY *(His eyes are closed and he suddenly starts to sing the opening lines of "Chattanooga Choo-Choo" with practically full voice)*

WYKOWSKI  Wake him up! Wake him up, for crise sakes!
*(ROY kicks CARNEY in the chest with his foot. CARNEY jumps)*

CARNEY  What the hell's wrong with you?

SELRIDGE  It's two-thirty in the goddamn morning. You were singing again.

CARNEY  I was not.

SELRIDGE  What do you mean, "You was not"? You practically made a record.

CARNEY  What was I singing?

SELRIDGE  "Chattanooga Choo-Choo."

CARNEY  I don't even know the words to "Chattanooga Choo-Choo."

5

WYKOWSKI  Maybe not awake. But you know them when you're sleeping.

CARNEY  *(To* EUGENE*)*  Hey, Gene. Was I singing "Chattanooga Choo-Choo"?

EUGENE  Yeah.

CARNEY  . . . Was I good?

EUGENE  Well, for a guy who was sleeping, it wasn't bad.

CARNEY  Damn. I wish I heard it.

EUGENE  *(To the audience)*  Donald Carney from Montclair, New Jersey, was an okay guy until someone made the fatal mistake of telling him he sounded like Perry Como. His voice was flat but his sister wasn't. She had the biggest breasts I ever saw. She came to visit him at Fort Dix wearing a tight red sweater and that's when I first discovered Wykowski's condition.
  *(The train rumbles on)*

WYKOWSKI  *(Sits up)*  goddamn it. Someone let go again . . . Was it you, Carney?

CARNEY  I was singing, wasn't I? I'm not going to do that while I'm singing.

WYKOWSKI  Yeah? Well, maybe you sang to cover it up.

SELRIDGE  Wait a minute. Wait a minute. *(He looks up)* It's coming from up there.
  *(They all look up.* EPSTEIN *has been sleeping on the grilling of the baggage rack with his rear end to the audience.* WYKOWSKI *whacks his cap hard against* EPSTEIN*'s butt)*

6

WYKOWSKI  Hey! Bombardier! Kill Germans, not G.I.s.
(EPSTEIN *turns around. He is slight of build*)

EPSTEIN  I'm sorry. I'm not feeling very well.

SELRIDGE  Yeah? Well, now we're *all* not feeling very well.

EUGENE  Leave him alone. He didn't do it on purpose.

SELRIDGE  (*To* EPSTEIN)  You hear, Epstein? He's your buddy. Aim the next one at him, okay?

EPSTEIN  Does anyone have an Alka-Seltzer tablet?

WYKOWSKI  Plugging it up ain't gonna help, Epstein.
(*He and* ROY *laugh. They all go back to their sleeping positions*)

EUGENE  (*Stops writing and looks at the audience*)  Arnold Epstein of Queens Boulevard, New York, was a sensitive, well-read, intelligent young man. His major flaw was that he was incapable of digesting food stronger than hard-boiled eggs . . . I didn't think he'd last long in the army because during wartime it's very hard to go home for dinner every night . . . (*The train rumbles on*) Hey, Arnold! What's the best book you ever read?

EPSTEIN  *War and Peace* . . . The fifth time.

EUGENE  If I wanted to become a writer, who do you recommend I read?

EPSTEIN  The entire third floor of the New York Public Library.

WYKOWSKI  Hey, Epstein? Can you read lips? Read this!
(*He gives Epstein a Bronx cheer.* SELRIDGE *laughs*)

EUGENE *(To the audience)* If the Germans only knew what was coming over, they would be looking forward to this invasion ... I'm Eugene Morris Jerome of Brighton Beach, Brooklyn, New York, and you can tell I've never been away from home before. In my duffel bag are twelve pot roast sandwiches my mother gave me ... There were three things I was determined to do in this war. Become a writer, not get killed, and lose my virginity ... But first I had to get through basic training in the murky swamps of Mississippi ...

*(There is silence for a moment, then* CARNEY, *eyes closed, begins to sing "Paper Doll." Lights dim as the train rumbles on. As* CARNEY's *singing slowly fades, we hear the sound of men marching and chanting out the cadence rhythms so familiar in the military.*

*Lights come up in the barracks as the sound of marching men fades.*

EUGENE, WYKOWSKI, EPSTEIN, SELRIDGE *and* CARNEY *amble into the barracks carrying their heavy barracks bags. They are hot, sweaty and tired. They look around at their new "home" for the next few months)*

EUGENE Boy, it's hot. This is hot! I am really hot! Oh, God, is it hot!

*(He puts his duffel in a lower bunk)*

WYKOWSKI You can cool off on the top 'cause that's *my* bunk down there.

*(He throws* EUGENE's *duffel on top and throws his own on the lower.* EPSTEIN *throws his duffel on the top bunk next to* EUGENE. *He looks at the rolled-up mattress and picks off a bedbug. They have all put their duffels on bunks and sit or lie down)*

CARNEY  I'm so tired I'm just gonna sleep on the springs.

EUGENE  It never got this hot in Brooklyn. This is like Africa-hot. *Tarzan* couldn't take this kind of hot.

SELRIDGE  Where's the phone? Call the manager. There's no ice water.

SERGEANT TOOMEY *(Enters with a clipboard)*  Dee-tail, attenSHUN!!
  *(The boys slowly get to their feet)*

SELRIDGE  Hi, Sarge.

TOOMEY  I think it's in your best interests, men, to move your asses when I yell ATTENSHUN!! MOVE IT!!! I want a single line right there! *(They all jump and line up in front of their bunks.* TOOMEY *paces up and down the line, looking them over)* Until the order "At Ease," is given, gentlemen, you are not "At Ease," is that understood? 'Tenshun! *(They snap to attention. He looks at them a moment)* At Ease! *(They stand "At Ease" . . .* TOOMEY *looks them over, then consults his clipboard)* Answer when your name is called. The answer to that question is "Ho." Not yes, not here, not right, not sir or any other unacceptable form of reply except the aforementioned "Ho," am I understood? Wykowski, Joseph T.

WYKOWSKI  Ho!

TOOMEY  Selridge, Roy W.

ROY  Ho!

TOOMEY  Carney, Donald J.

CARNEY  Ho!

TOOMEY  Jerome, Eugene M.

EUGENE  Ho!

TOOMEY  Epstein, Arnold B.

EPSTEIN  Ho Ho!
    (TOOMEY *looks at him*)

TOOMEY  Are there two Arnold Epsteins in this company?

EPSTEIN  No, Sergeant.

TOOMEY  Then just give me one goddamn Ho.

EPSTEIN  Yes, Sergeant.

TOOMEY  Epstein, Arnold B.

EPSTEIN  Ho!

TOOMEY  One more time.

EPSTEIN  Ho!

TOOMEY  Let me hear it again.

EPSTEIN  Ho!

TOOMEY  Am I understood?

EPSTEIN  Ho!  (*as if to say "Of course"*)

EUGENE  (*To the audience*)  Arnold Epstein was the worst soldier in World War Two and that included the deserters . . . He just refused to show respect to those he thought were his intellectual inferiors.

TOOMEY  (*To the men*)  . . . My name is Toomey, Sergeant Merwin J. Toomey, and I am in charge of C Company during your ten weeks of basic training here in Beautiful Biloxi, Mississippi, after which those of you who have survived the heat, humidity, roaches, spiders, snakes, dry rot, fungus, dysentery, syphilis, gonorrhea and tick fever will be sent to some shit island in the Pacific or some turd pile in Northern Sicily. In either case, returning to your mommas and poppas with your balls intact is highly improbable. There's only one way to come out of a war healthy of body and sane of mind and that way is to be born the favorite daughter of the President of the United States . . . I speak from experience, having served fourteen months in the North African campaign where seventy-three percent of my comrades are buried under the sand of an A-rab desert. The colorful ribbons on my chest will testify to the fact that my government is grateful for my contribution having donated a small portion of my brains to this conflict, the other portion being protected by a heavy steel plate in my head. This injury has caused me to become a smart, compassionate, understanding and sympathetic teacher of raw, young men—or the cruelest, craziest, most sadistic goddamn son of a bitch you ever saw . . . and that's something you won't know until ten weeks from now, do I make myself clear, Epstein?

EPSTEIN  I think so.

TOOMEY  DO I MAKE MYSELF CLEAR, EP-STEIN??

EPSTEIN  Ho!

TOOMEY  DO I MAKE MYSELF CLEAR, JEROME?

EUGENE  Ho yes!

TOOMEY  Ho *what*?

EUGENE  Ho nothing.

TOOMEY  Goddamn right, boy.

EUGENE *(To the audience)*  I hated the lousy movies. I thought I was going to get a nice officer like James Stewart.

TOOMEY *(Looks at* EUGENE*)* Are you paying attention to me, Jerome?

EUGENE *(Nervously)* Yes ho. I mean Ho, sir. Just plain Ho.

TOOMEY Where are you from, Jerome?

EUGENE 1427 Pulaski Avenue.

TOOMEY In my twelve years in the army, I never met one goddamn dogface who came from 1427 Pulaski Avenue. Why is that, Jerome?

EUGENE Because it's my home. Only my family lives there. I'm sorry. I meant I live in Brighton Beach, Brooklyn, New York.

*(*TOOMEY *notices* EPSTEIN *shifting from foot to foot)*

TOOMEY Hey, Fred Astaire! You trying to tell me something?

EPSTEIN I have to go to the bathroom, Sergeant.

TOOMEY Now how are you going to do that? We don't have bathrooms in the army.

EPSTEIN They had them in Fort Dix.

TOOMEY Not bathrooms, they didn't.

EPSTEIN Yes, they did, Sergeant. I went in them a lot.

TOOMEY Well, I'm telling you we don't have any bathrooms on this base. Do you doubt my veracity?

EPSTEIN No, Sergeant.

TOOMEY Then you've got a problem, haven't you, Epstein?

EPSTEIN Ho ho.

TOOMEY You bet your ass, ho ho . . . Do you know why you've got a problem, Epstein?

EPSTEIN Because I have to go real bad.

TOOMEY  No, son. You've got a problem because you don't know army terminology. The place where a U.S. soldier goes to defecate, relieve himself, open his bowels, shit, fart, dump, crap and unload is called the latrine. La-trine! (EUGENE *smiles*) Want to tell us what's funny about that, Jerome?

EUGENE  Well . . . that you said all those words in one sentence.

TOOMEY  That's why these ribbons are pinned on my shirt. Because I'm an experienced army man. Do you understand that, Jerome?

EUGENE  Ha.

TOOMEY  What?

EUGENE  Ho.

TOOMEY  Where are you from, Wykowski?

WYKOWSKI  Bridgeport, Connecticut.

TOOMEY  Do you know where that is, Selridge?

SELRIDGE  It's er . . . in Connecticut. Bridgeport, I think.

TOOMEY  Is that right, Wykowski?

WYKOWSKI  Ho.

TOOMEY  (*Looks directly at* ROY)  And what did you do in Bridgeport, soldier?

SELRIDGE  I was never there, Sergeant.

TOOMEY  I wasn't talking to you, Selridge.

SELRIDGE  Oh. You were looking at me.

TOOMEY  I may be looking at you but I am talking to the soldier from Bridgeport. (*He looks into* ROY'*s face*) Now, what did you do there, Wykowski?
  (*They all look confused*)

13

WYKOWSKI   I drove a truck. A moving van. I was a furniture mover.

TOOMEY   That's just what they need in the South Pacific, Wykowski. Someone who knows how to move furniture around in the jungle. (EPSTEIN *half raises his hand*) I believe Private Epstein has a question.

EPSTEIN   May I go to the latrine, Sergeant?

TOOMEY   No. I am addressing the new members of my company, Epstein. (*He looks directly into* WYKOWSKI's *face*) What's your name again, soldier?

WYKOWSKI   Wykowski.

TOOMEY   I am talking to the man next to you.

SELRIDGE   Selridge!

TOOMEY (*Points to* CARNEY)   *You*, boy! You are the one I am directing my question to.

CARNEY   Carney, sir. Donald J . . . Ho!

TOOMEY   I didn't ask if you were here. I can *see* that you're here. I asked where you're from, Carney, Donald J.

CARNEY (*Thinks*)   I don't remember . . . Er, Montclair, New Jersey.

TOOMEY   And what was your civilian occupation in Montclair, New Jersey, Private Carney, Donald J.?

CARNEY   I didn't have any.

TOOMEY   No occupation? You were unemployed then, is that right?

CARNEY   No, Sergeant. I worked in a shoe store. In the stock room.

TOOMEY (*Stares at him*)   Did I not hear you just say you didn't have an occupation?

CARNEY  Not in Montclair. I *lived* in Montclair. I worked in Teaneck. You just asked what my occupation was in Montclair.

TOOMEY  I see ... Is it your intention, Private Carney, Donald J., to humiliate and ridicule me in front of my company?

CARNEY  No, Sergeant.

TOOMEY  And yet that is precisely what you did. As I stand here in front of my newly arrived company, you took this opportunity, assuming that because of my Southern heritage, I was an uneducated and illiterate cotton picker, you purposefully and deliberately humiliated me. Did you think for one second you would get away with that, Private Carney, Donald J.?

CARNEY  I wasn't trying to get away with—

TOOMEY  Well, I can assure you, YOU DID NOT AND WILL NOT! You just got your ass in a sling, boy! *Does everyone understand that?*

ALL TOGETHER  HO!!!

TOOMEY  What?

ALL TOGETHER *(Louder)*  HO!!!

TOOMEY  I am, strictly speaking, Carney, old army. And old army means discipline. Can you do push-ups, Private Carney?

CARNEY  Yes, Sergeant.

TOOMEY  What is the highest total of push-ups you ever achieved in one session, Private Carney?

CARNEY  I'm not too strong in the arms. About ten ... maybe fifteen.

TOOMEY   Congratulations, Carney. You are about to break your old record. I want one hundred push-ups from you, Carney, and I want them *now*. AM I UNDERSTOOD?

CARNEY   One hundred? Oh, I couldn't possibly do one hu—

TOOMEY   HIT THE FLOOR, SOLDIER!!!

CARNEY   I could do, say, twenty a day for five days—

TOOMEY   Count off, goddammit, and move your ass!

CARNEY   (*Starts doing push-ups*) One . . . two . . . three . . . four . . . five . . .

TOOMEY   (*Looks into* EPSTEIN's *eyes*) Nobody eats, drinks, sleeps or goes to the latrine until I hear one hundred.

CARNEY   Six . . . seven . . .   Oh, God . . . nine . . . ten . . .

TOOMEY   Eight. You forgot eight, didn't you, boy?

CARNEY   I did it. I just didn't say it.

TOOMEY   Well, say them all, Donny boy. Let's start again from one. Let's hear it.

CARNEY   One . . . two . . . three . . .
         (CARNEY *continues this throughout the scene with great difficulty*)

TOOMEY   (*Shouting*) *Private Jerome!* Do you think this is cruel, unfair and unjust punishment being inflicted on Private Carney?

EUGENE   Oh, gee, I don't know. It's my first day—

TOOMEY   I want the God Almighty truth from you. Is this punishment unfair and unjust, Private Jerome?

EUGENE *(To the audience)*  If only I had a heart murmur, I wouldn't be in this trouble.

TOOMEY  Your answer, boy.

EUGENE  Well, I think it was a misunderstanding . . . I think er—*(He feels his head)* I think I have swamp fever, sir.

TOOMEY  Yes or no, Jerome. Am I being unfair to the young man who is breaking his ass on the floor?

EUGENE  In my opinion? . . . Yes, Sergeant.

TOOMEY  I see . . . Apparently, Jerome, you don't understand the benefits of discipline. It is discipline that will win this war for us. Therefore, until you learn it, soldier, I will just have to keep teaching it to you . . . *Selridge!* One hundred push-ups. *Hit* the floor!

SELRIDGE  Me??? . . . I didn't say nothin'.

TOOMEY  When we do battle, we are sometimes called upon to sacrifice ourselves for the sake of others.

SELRIDGE  Yeah, but we didn't do battle yet.

TOOMEY  ON YOUR FACE, SOLDIER!!

SELRIDGE *(On the floor)*  One . . . two . . . three . . . four . . . five . . .
*(They continue)*

TOOMEY *(To* EUGENE*)*  What I have done to Private Selridge may seem even more unfair and unjust than what I did to Private Carney. Is that your opinion, Private Jerome?

EUGENE *(Takes a deep breath)*  . . . No, Sergeant.

TOOMEY  Hold it, boys. *(To the others; they stop)* You all heard that. Private Jerome approves of my method of discipline. He thinks what I am doing is fair, moral and just. Therefore, with his approval and endorsement, Private Wykowski will join us for one hundred push-ups. Hit the deck, Wykowski! I can see how grateful you are. You can thank your buddy, Private Jerome.

WYKOWSKI *(Glaring at* EUGENE*)*   I will. Later.
*(He starts push-ups)*

TOOMEY   Back to work, boys.

WYKOWSKI   One . . . two . . . three . . . four . . .

EUGENE *(To* WYKOWSKI*)*   I'm sorry.
(CARNEY *is struggling)*

CARNEY   I—I don't think I can do any more, Sergeant.

TOOMEY   I realize that, son, and I sympathize with you. If only there were some way I could help you.

EUGENE   I could finish it for him, Sergeant.

TOOMEY   That's damn decent of you, Jerome, but I think Private Carney doesn't expect other men to shoulder his responsibility.

CARNEY   I would be willing to make an exception, Sergeant.

TOOMEY   What I think you need, Carney, is inspiration. Therefore, I am asking volunteers to join Privates Carney, Selridge and Wykowski on the barracks floor. All volunteers take one step forward and shout, "Ho!" Sound off!

EUGENE *(Takes one step forward)*   Ho!
(EPSTEIN *remains silent and doesn't move)*

TOOMEY   We have one volunteer . . . and one inconclusive. *(He turns to* EPSTEIN *and moves in face to face)*

Does your silence mean you are not volunteering, Private Epstein?

EPSTEIN   I have a slight deformity of the spine which escaped the medical exam—

TOOMEY   ON YOUR FACE, EPSTEIN!!! (ARNOLD *drops to the floor*) Ready . . . Ho!

EPSTEIN   One . . . two . . . three . . . four . . .
*(All four men are doing push-ups.* CARNEY *and* EP-STEIN *struggle the most.*
TOOMEY *paces back and forth, nodding happily)*

TOOMEY   Now we're moving ahead in our quest for discipline . . . As the sweat pours off your brows and your puny muscles strain to lift your flabby, chubby, jellied bodies, think of Private Jerome of Brighton Beach, New York, who is *not* down there beside you. *Not* sharing your pain, *not* sharing your struggle . . . Fate always chooses someone to get a free ride. The kind of man who always gets away with all kinds of shit. In this company it seems to be Private Eugene M. Jerome. Eventually we get to hate those men. Hate them, loathe them and despise them. How does Private Jerome learn to deal with this cold wall of anger and hostility? By learning to endure it alone. That, gentlemen, is the supreme lesson in discipline. You're slowing down, boys. The sooner you finish, the sooner you'll get to our fine Southern cooking . . . Up down . . . Up down . . . Carry on instructions, Jerome. Up down . . . up down . . .
*(*TOOMEY *leaves)*

EUGENE   *(To the audience)*   It was then I decided I had to get out of the Army . . . I thought of shooting off

a part of my body I might not need in later life but
I couldn't find any . . . But the worst was still to
come . . .
  (*Lights out on* EUGENE.

  *Lights up on a section of the mess hall.* WYKOWSKI,
  SELRIDGE, CARNEY *and* EPSTEIN *are sitting at a
  wooden table, staring frozen-faced at the aluminum
  tray filled with "supper" in front of them. Nobody
  moves. The forks in their hands are raised motionless
  above the tray*)

CARNEY  What do you think it is?

WYKOWSKI  My brother had this in the marines. It's
S.O.S.

CARNEY  What's S.O.S.?

WYKOWSKI  Shit on a shingle.

CARNEY  (*Inspecting it*)  Yeah, that's what it looks like
all right.

SELRIDGE  What do you mean? They take a shingle
and they put—shit on it?

WYKOWSKI  It's beef. Creamed chipped beef.

EPSTEIN  Why would you chip something after it's
been creamed?

WYKOWSKI  It doesn't look so bad to me. Hell, I'm
hungry. (*He takes a forkful and eats it. They all watch
him*) . . . It's terrific . . . It needs ketchup, that's
all.
  (*He puts ketchup on it*)

SELRIDGE  They oughta drop this stuff over Germany.
The whole country would come out with their
hands up.
  (EUGENE *appears, carrying his tray. His mouth is*

*agape, his face aghast as he looks at what's on his tray)*

EUGENE   I saw this in the Bronx Zoo. The gorillas were throwing it at each other.

EPSTEIN   If you can't eat this, you can get something else. It's government regulations. Enlisted men must be served palatable food.

WYKOWSKI   Why don't you ask them for some matzoh ball soup, Epstein. I hear the army makes great matzoh ball soup.
*(He and* SELRIDGE *laugh.* EUGENE *looks emphatically at* EPSTEIN)

EPSTEIN   It's my right to speak up. *(He looks around)* I'm going to speak to the sergeant.

CARNEY   Sit down, would you, please?

EUGENE   Don't start in with him, Arnold. He's crazy. This was probably his recipe.

WYKOWSKI *(To* EUGENE *and* EPSTEIN)   Listen, you two guys. Don't give the sergeant any more crap. 'Cause when he doesn't like you, he doesn't like the rest of us. Any guy who screws up in this platoon is in deep shit with me, understand?

EPSTEIN   Who made you lieutenant colonel?

WYKOWSKI   *I* did. I promoted myself. If I have to do any more push-ups on account of you, Epstein, you're going to be underneath me when I'm doing them.

SELRIDGE   Well, now we know who the fruits are.
*(He laughs)*

EPSTEIN   I'm not even supposed to be in the army with my stomach. No one's going to make me eat this if I don't want to.

(JAMES HENNESEY, *a soldier their own age, on KP,
comes over to refill their sugar jars*)

HENNESEY You guys hear what happened over at
Baker Company? Some kid went nuts. Said he was
going home, didn't want no part of this army. An
officer tried to stop him and the kid belted him one,
broke the Captain's nose. They said this guy's sure
to get five to ten years in Leavenworth. They don't
crap around in the army, you find that out real
fast.

CARNEY I hope they ship us out to the Pacific. At least
we'd get Chinese food.

HENNESEY My name is Hennesey. I'm in your platoon. They gave me eight straight days of KP.

WYKOWSKI How come?

HENNESEY I left over two spoonfuls of barley soup.
Two lousy spoonfuls . . . Be careful, you guys.
(*He turns and moves away quickly as* SGT. TOOMEY
*approaches the table*)

TOOMEY How my boys doing? (*All except* EPSTEIN *smile
and greet him warmly*) How's the chow?

WYKOWSKI (*Sounding overly cheerful*) First rate, Sarge.

SELRIDGE They don't give you enough.

EUGENE Surprisingly interesting food, Sarge.

TOOMEY Not hungry, Epstein?

EPSTEIN I find enough nourishment in bread and
water, Sergeant.

TOOMEY Well, you're all going to need plenty of
nourishment with ten back-breaking weeks ahead of
us, starting tonight.

CARNEY Tonight?

TOOMEY   Worked out a little surprise for you. Something to work off tonight's dinner. We're going on a midnight hike, men.

EUGENE   Midnight?

TOOMEY   Not too far, this being your first night in camp. Just a short fifteen-mile walk around the marshes and swamps. How does that sound to you, Jerome? You think that's a reasonable request of me to make?

EUGENE   We've sort of elected Wykowski our leader. I think he should answer that.
         (WYKOWSKI *glares at* EUGENE)

TOOMEY   Is that right, Wykowski?

WYKOWSKI   I don't question orders, Sergeant. I just follow them.

TOOMEY   That's a good answer, Wykowski. It's a chicken-shit one, but a good answer . . . How about you, Epstein? You up to a fifteen-mile walk around the swamp?

EPSTEIN   . . . No, Sergeant.

TOOMEY   No??? Epstein's not up to it, men . . . Why is that, Epstein?

EPSTEIN   We've been on a train for five days and five nights. We haven't had one good night's sleep since we left Fort Dix.

TOOMEY   I see . . . Okay. Fair enough, Epstein . . . You're excused from the hike. I appreciate a man who speaks up.

EPSTEIN   Thank you, Sergeant.

TOOMEY   You get a good night's sleep just as soon as you've washed, scrubbed and shined every john, uri-

23

nal and basin in the latrine. If it doesn't sparkle when we get back, then Wykowski and Selridge are going to do two hundred push-ups. That'll put you in good with the boys, Epstein . . . Anyone else care to stay home for the evening? . . . Okay then, let's get moving. Full field packs in front of barracks at twenty-four hundred hours, ready to march. LET'S GET CRACKING! *(They all jump up, except EP-STEIN)* HOLD ON ONE GODDAMN MINUTE!!! *(They all stop)* Nobody—but NOBODY—leaves here with good U.S. Army chow untouched, uneaten and unfinished. You can sit there poking at it with your fork till it sprouts weeds, but by God, you will sit there until that tray is empty . . . Line up in front of me, trays extended for inspection. *(They quickly line up in front of* TOOMEY *in single file.* WYKOWSKI *is first.* TOOMEY *looks into his tray)* Okay, Wykowski, move! *(*SELRIDGE *is next)* Right, Selridge, move. *(He follows* WYKOWSKI *out.* CARNEY *is next. His food is untouched)* Something wrong with your dinner, Carney?

CARNEY    Yes, Sarge. It's the first food I was ever afraid of.

TOOMEY    You'll like it about a month from now 'cause that's how long you'll be sitting there. Back to your seat! *(*CARNEY *glumly goes back and sits at the table.* EUGENE *steps in front of* TOOMEY, *tray extended)* Don't approve of our *cuisine,* Jerome?

EUGENE    It's not that, Sarge. It's a religious objection. This is the week that my people fast for two days.

TOOMEY    This is March, Jerome. Rosh-Ahonah and Yom Kippur are in September. I have an all-religion calendar in my barracks room. Don't you try that shit on me again!

EUGENE  It's a different holiday. It's called El Malagueña.

TOOMEY  El Malagueña??

EUGENE  It's for Spanish Jews.

TOOMEY  Carney!

CARNEY  Yes, Sarge?

TOOMEY  Put half your tray onto Jerome's.

CARNEY *(Smiles)*  Yes, Sergeant.

TOOMEY *(To EUGENE)*  Eat in good health, Jerome, and Happy El Malagueña to you. (CARNEY *eagerly scrapes half his tray into* EUGENE'S. EUGENE, *looking miserable, sits.* EPSTEIN *steps in front of* TOOMEY) Okay, Epstein, what's your story? And don't tell me today is La Coocharacha.

EPSTEIN  I have a legitimate excuse, Sergeant. I have a digestive disorder, diagnosed as a nervous stomach.

TOOMEY  Is that right? And how come you passed the army medical examination?

EPSTEIN  It only gets nervous while I'm eating food. I wasn't eating food during the examination. I brought a chicken salad sandwich along to show them what happens when it enters the digestive tract . . .

TOOMEY  Are you a psycho, Epstein? You sound like a psycho to me. That's a psycho story.

EPSTEIN *(Reaches into his breast pocket)*  I have a letter from my internist who's on the staff of Mount Sinai Hospital on Fifth Avenue—

(TOOMEY *grabs the letter from* EPSTEIN *and quickly reads it*)

TOOMEY  Did you show this to the army medical examining officer?

EPSTEIN  Yes, Sergeant.

TOOMEY  What did he say?

EPSTEIN  He said don't eat chicken salad sandwiches and then he accepted me.

TOOMEY  Then this letter ain't worth the paper it's written on. (*He tears it up and shreds it over* EPSTEIN'S *food*) I expect to see everything on that tray gone, Epstein, including that letter. The corporal at the door will be watching you. Good appetite, men. (*Turns briskly and starts out*) "El Malagueña" . . .

(EPSTEIN *sits, and the three men sit in stony silence*)

EUGENE  I've got an idea.

CARNEY  Yeah?

EUGENE  We dump it under the table. We'll be gone by the time they find it.

CARNEY  Great idea. But we have to time it right. When no one's looking.

EUGENE  I'll tell you when.

CARNEY  Remember. Timing's everything.

EUGENE (*Looks around*)  . . . Okay. *Now!*
(*In unison they lower their trays under the table. They are about to dump the food when the voice of the* CORPORAL *calls out*)

VOICE (*Sharp*)  GET THOSE TRAYS BACK ON THE TABLE.
(*They bring trays quickly back up*)

CARNEY  . . . Work on your timing.

EPSTEIN  Give it to me.

CARNEY  What?

EPSTEIN  I'm not going to eat mine. No point in all of us suffering. Scrape it onto my tray.

EUGENE  You mean it?

EPSTEIN  This is lunacy. I'm an intelligent human being. I refuse to capitulate to the lunatics. One day when this war is over, there will be investigations . . . *(To the boys)* Go on. Give it to me.
*(They scrape their food onto* EPSTEIN's *tray)*

CARNEY  I like you, Epstein, but you're weird as hell . . . But I'll tell you one thing. I'm sitting next to you every meal we get.
*(He leaves)*

EUGENE  I could have used you when my mother made lima beans.
*(He leaves)*

EPSTEIN  . . . I won't eat slop . . . I won't eat slop . . . I WON'T EAT SLOP! I WON'T EAT SLOP!

EUGENE *(Appears in field equipment)*  . . . Arnold didn't eat the slop. They gave him K.P. for five straight days including cleaning the latrines. But that was better than the midnight march through the murky swamps of Mississippi. *(We hear the sound of eerie birds and strange animals.* EUGENE *looks up)* The only time I heard strange sounds like that was at Ebbets Field when the Dodgers played . . . Toomey made Wykowski carry me the whole fifteen miles just so Wykowski would hate me more . . . But maybe Toomey was right. If nobody obeys orders, I'll bet

27

we wouldn't have more than twelve or thirteen soldiers fighting the war . . . We'd have headlines like,
"Corporal Stanley Leiberman invades Sicily" . . .
*(Lights off on* EUGENE. *Lights up on the barracks.* EPSTEIN
*enters from the latrine,* EUGENE *goes to his locker)* Hey,
Arnold, it was incredible. You missed it. We were
in the swamps up to our necks. There were water
snakes and big lizards that crawled up your pants
and swooping swamp birds that swooped down and
went right for your eyeballs . . . What's wrong,
Arnold? . . . Arnold? . . .

EPSTEIN *(Sitting down)* Leave me alone!

EUGENE What is it? Are you sick?

EPSTEIN Get away from me. You're like all the rest of
them. I hate every goddamn one of you.

EUGENE Hey, Arnold, I'm your friend. I'm your
buddy. You can talk to me.

EPSTEIN *(Sits up and looks around)* . . . I'm getting out.
I'm leaving in the morning. I'm going to Mexico or
Central America till after the war . . . I will not be
treated like dirt, like a maggot. I'm not going to help
defend a country that won't even defend its own
citizens . . . Bastards!

EUGENE Because you pulled latrine duty? We all have
to pull latrine duty. You have to adjust . . . It's all
a game, Arnold. Only it's their ball and their rules.
And they know the game better than we do because
they've been playing it since Valley Forge.

EPSTEIN . . . I was in the latrine alone. I spent four
hours cleaning it, on my hands and knees. It looked
better than my mother's bathroom at home. Then

these two non-coms come in, one was the cook, that
three-hundred-pound guy and some other slob,
with cigar butts in their mouths and reeking from
beer . . . They come in to pee only instead of using
the urinal, they use one of the johns, both peeing in
the same one, making circles, figure-eights. Then
they start to walk out and I say, "Hey, I just cleaned
that. Please flush the johns." And the big one, the
cook, says to me, "Up your ass, rookie," or some
other really clever remark . . . And I block the door-
way and I say, "There's a printed order on the wall
signed by Captain Landon stating the regulations
that all facilities must be flushed after using" . . .
And I'm requesting that they follow regulations,
since I was left in charge, and to please flush the
facility . . . And the big one says to me, "Suppose
you flush it, New York Jew Kike," and I said, "My
ethnic heritage notwithstanding, please flush the facility" . . . They look at each other, this half a ton
of brainless beef, and suddenly rush me, turn me
upside down, grab my ankles and—and—and they
lowered me by my feet with my head in the toilet,
in their filth, their poison . . . all the way until I
couldn't breathe . . . then they pulled off my belt and
tied my feet on to the ceiling pipes with my head
still in their foul waste and tied my hands behind
my back with dirty rags, and they left me there,
hanging like a pig that was going to be slaughtered
. . . I wasn't strong enough to fight back. I couldn't
do it alone. No one came to help me . . . Then the
pipe broke and I fell to the ground . . . It took me
twenty minutes to get myself untied—twenty minutes!—but it will take me the rest of my life to wash
off my humiliation. I was degraded. I lost my dig-

nity. If I stay, Gene, if they put a gun in my hands, one night, I swear to God, I'll kill them both . . . I'm not a murderer. I don't want to disgrace my family . . . But I have to get out of here . . . Now do you understand?

EUGENE   But you can't go AWOL. They'll catch you. They have agents all over the world . . . You'll get back at them one day. Don't you believe in justice?

EPSTEIN   . . . You're so damn naïve, Eugene.

(WYKOWSKI *and* SELRIDGE *come out of the latrine in their underwear, carrying towels, toothbrushes and toothpaste*)

WYKOWSKI (*Scratching*)   I got a hundred and twelve goddamn mosquito bites.

SELRIDGE (*Shivering*)   I pulled twelve leeches off me. I pulled one off near my crotch, it wasn't a leech. Maybe I pulled something else off.

(*He gets into bed, still shivering.* CARNEY *and* HENNESEY *come out in their underwear, towels*)

CARNEY   I heard a top-secret rumor today. I'm not supposed to repeat it.

WYKOWSKI   What is it?

CARNEY   I can get in trouble if it gets out.

WYKOWSKI   No one's gonna talk. What is it?

CARNEY   I hear they're getting ready to invade Europe and Japan on the same day.

HENNESEY   Where'd you hear that?

CARNEY   On the radio. It was one of them small stations.

EUGENE   Why on the same day?

CARNEY    Surprise attack. You hit them both at dawn. Then they don't have enough time to warn each other.

EUGENE    Hey, Carney. When it's dawn in Europe, it's a day later in Japan. They don't have dawn at the same time. Japan could read about it in their newspapers.

HENNESEY    Besides, we're not ready. We don't have enough trained men to invade both places on the same day.

EPSTEIN    You know what *Time* magazine estimates the casualty rate of a full-scale invasion would be? Sixty-eight percent. Sixty-eight percent of us would be killed or wounded.

WYKOWSKI    No shit? . . . So out of this group, how many is that?

EPSTEIN    Of the six of us here, about four point three of us would get it.

CARNEY    What part of your body is point three?

SELRIDGE    Hey, Wykowski. We know what part of *your* body is point three.
    (*He giggles*)

EUGENE    Listen, if you knew you were one of the guys who wasn't coming back, if you knew it right now, what would you do with the last few days of your life? It could be anything you want . . . I give everyone five seconds to think about it.

CARNEY    I thought about it. I'm not dying. You think I'm gonna kill myself to entertain *you?*

EUGENE  Why not? It's like a fantasy. I'm giving you the opportunity to do anything in the world you ever dreamed of . . . Come on.

SELRIDGE  I think it's a good idea. Let's play for money.

HENNESEY  For *money?*

SELRIDGE  Yeah. Five bucks a man. The guy with the best fantasy collects the pot.

HENNESEY  That's morbid.

WYKOWSKI  Okay, I'm in. We need a judge.

EUGENE  I'll be the judge.

WYKOWSKI  Why you?

EUGENE  Because I thought of the game. Ante up, everyone. Come on, Hennesey. *(They all put up money except* EPSTEIN*)* Come on, Arnold. I *know* you have some great fantasies.

EPSTEIN  I don't sell my fantasies.

WYKOWSKI  Burn his bunk!

EUGENE  Come on, Arnold . . . for me.

SELRIDGE  I love this. I'm gonna clean up.

EUGENE  *(Jubilantly)* Okay, Carney. You're first. You're dead. Killed in action . . . What would you do with your last days on earth?

CARNEY  How much time do I have to do it in?

EUGENE  A week.

SELRIDGE  I need ten days.

EUGENE  It's my game. You only get a week . . . What would you do with it, Donny?

CARNEY *(Thinks)* Okay . . . I would sing at the Radio City Music Hall. Five shows a day, my own spot. In the audience are four thousand girls and one man. Every girl is gorgeous. Every girl is size 38-24-36 . . . And they all want me . . . real bad.

HENNESEY Who's the man?

CARNEY The President of Decca Records. He wants me too. I have a choice. After the last show, I could have all four thousand girls . . . or a contract with Decca Records.

HENNESEY Which one do you take?

SELRIDGE *(Urging him on)* The record contract. I would take the record contract.

CARNEY Right. I take the record contract.

SELRIDGE *(Laughs)* MORON!! He believed me. He could have humped four thousand girls and now he's got a record contract that ain't worth shit.

CARNEY Wrong! Because now I'm a big star and stars get all the girls they want anyway.

SELRIDGE Yeah? How? You're dead. Girls never go out with dead record stars.

CARNEY Bullshit! I paid five bucks for my fantasy. I can do what I want . . . What's my score, Gene?

EUGENE Well, you started off with an A-minus but you finished with a B.

CARNEY B. Not bad—better than I ever did in school.

EUGENE All right. Selridge is next.

SELRIDGE Okay . . . Here we go . . . I make it with the seven richest women in the world. And I'm so hot, each dame gives me a million bucks. And at the end of a week, I got seven million bucks. Pretty good, heh?

EUGENE    If you're dead, what are you going to do with seven million dollars?

SELRIDGE    I told you. That's why I need ten days. I need a long weekend to spend the money. Give up, suckers, I got you all beat.

EPSTEIN    Moronic. It's beyond moronic. It's sub-moronic.

SELRIDGE    Break their hearts, Jerome, and tell 'em my score.

EUGENE    It lacks poetry. I give Selridge a B.

SELRIDGE *(Angrily)*    A *B*? You give me a B? That creep signs a record contract that ain't worth shit and he gets a B? *(He heads for the money)* I want my money back.

WYKOWSKI    Touch that money and you're dead.

SELRIDGE    I was kidding. You think I was serious? I was kidding. *(He lies on his bunk)* Who's next?

EUGENE    Hennesey.

HENNESEY    Me? I'm not ready yet.

EUGENE    It's your turn.

HENNESEY    I'm not good at things like this.

EUGENE    Come on. Just say it.

HENNESEY    I can't think of anything.

SELRIDGE    He can't think of anything. So he's out. Tough shit. Give him an F . . . Who's next?

HENNESEY    Okay. Okay . . . I'd spend it with my family.

WYKOWSKI  Is this guy serious?

CARNEY  Damn, I wish we were playing for big dough.

SELRIDGE  What an asshole.

HENNESEY  It's my last week. I can spend it any way I want. I'd like it to be with my family.

CARNEY *(Mimicking him)*  I'd like it to be with my family.

SELRIDGE  Go ahead, Jerome. What do you give him for *that* crap?

EUGENE  It's not interesting but at least it's honest . . . I give him a B-plus.

SELRIDGE  Okay. This game is fixed. I'm calling in the Military Police. I get a B for screwin' seven millionairesses and *he* gets a B-plus for goin' home to his mother? . . . I change my answer. I want to visit sick children in the hospital.

WYKOWSKI  Knock it off, Selridge. You had your turn.

EUGENE  It's yours now, Wykowski.

CARNEY  Don't let us down, Kowski. To some of us you're a hero.

WYKOWSKI  Okay . . . I always wanted to make it with a world-famous woman that nobody else could have. It didn't make no difference if she was beautiful or not, as long as I was the only one.

HENNESEY  Have you got someone in mind?

WYKOWSKI *(Smiling)*  Yeah. I got someone in mind.

EUGENE  I think we're heading for an A-plus.

CARNEY  Who's the woman, Kowski?

WYKOWSKI *(Does a grind and a bump)* . . . The Queen of England!
   *(They all stare at him, dumbstruck)*

CARNEY   The Queen of England????

SELRIDGE   That is disgusting. That's like making it with your grandmother.

EUGENE   Besides, you wouldn't be the only one. What about the *King* of England?

WYKOWSKI   Kings and Queens just do it once a year. To make a Prince. But I'd have her every day and every night for a week.

SELRIDGE   You couldn't get near her. They keep her under guard at Rockingham Palace.

WYKOWSKI   Not for me. She would say—*(In a high-pitched voice)* "Let that sexy Wykowski in my chamber."

EPSTEIN   Apes and gorillas. I'm living with apes and gorillas.

HENNESEY   What's his score? Give him his score.

CARNEY   *(In a high-pitched English voice)*   Yes. Give the Earl of Meatloaf his score.

EUGENE   This is a tough one. I find it completely unredeeming in every way. Morally, ethically and sexually . . . but it's got style . . . *A*-minus!

SELRIDGE   *(Furiously)*   Okay. I want my five bucks back. I'm not getting beat out by a guy who humps the Mother of the British Empire.

HENNESEY   Boy, I'm learning a lot about you guys tonight.

SELRIDGE   And versa visa, jerk-off.

WYKOWSKI  So I'm winning, right?

EUGENE  It's not over yet. There's two more to go.

SELRIDGE  Epstein's next. I want to hear what *his* last
week on earth would be like. Probably wants to take
an English exam at City College.

EUGENE  It's your turn, Arnold.

EPSTEIN  There's no point to this game.

EUGENE  Yes, there is.

EPSTEIN  What's the point?

EUGENE  I like it . . . Come on. It's your last week on
earth. You're going to get killed overseas. What's
your secret desire?
    *(They all look at* EPSTEIN *. . . He thinks carefully)*

EPSTEIN  . . . I don't want to say. If I say it, it might
not come true.

CARNEY  He doesn't have one. All he does is com-
plain.

WYKOWSKI  And pass gas. That's his secret desire. He
wants to bend over and blow up the world.
    *(*SELRIDGE *loves that one)*

EUGENE  Wait a minute. Give him a chance. He has
one . . . What is it, Arnold? What's the last thing you
want to do on this earth?
    *(All attention is on* EPSTEIN*)*

EPSTEIN  . . . I would like to make Sergeant Merwin
J. Toomey do two hundred push-ups in front of this
platoon.
    *(There is stunned silence)*

WYKOWSKI  That's good . . . I hate to admit it, but it's
good.

37

SELRIDGE   It's okay. Five hundred would have been better.

EUGENE   I think it's terrific. I give Epstein an A-plus.

CARNEY   A-plus? You're crazy. Now you can't beat him.

EUGENE   I can still tie him.

WYKOWSKI   If it's a tie, all bets are off. Nobody wins.

EUGENE   Fair enough. Somebody else has to judge me. Pick a judge, Wykowski.

WYKOWSKI   *(Smiles)*   Sure, I pick Selridge.

SELRIDGE   I love it. No matter what crap he says, he gets an A-plus. Your money is safe, boys.

HENNESEY   Go on, Gene . . . Let's hear yours.

EUGENE   Okay. *(He takes a deep breath. They listen intently)* . . . I'm going to get mine wiping out a whole battalion of Japanese marines. They'll put up a statue of me at Brighton Beach. *(He poses)* Maybe name a junior high school after me, or a swimming pool.

SELRIDGE   All they'd give you is a locker room. The Eugene M. Jerome Locker Room.

HENNESEY   Let him finish. Go on, Gene.

EUGENE   Well . . . if it's my last week on earth . . . I would like to fall in love.

CARNEY   With who?

EUGENE   The perfect girl.

WYKOWSKI   There is no perfect girl.

EUGENE   If I fell in love with her, she'd be perfect.

WYKOWSKI   I told you. Jewish guys are all homos.

CARNEY  Incredible! . . . Okay, the game is over. Tell him what he got, Roy, and we'll all take our money back.

(*They look at* SELRIDGE)

WYKOWSKI  Go on. Tell him his score.

SELRIDGE  I give him a C-minus.

WYKOWSKI  What??

SELRIDGE  I'm sorry. I'm not gonna let him beat me with that pissy story. I came up with something "hot," I'm not gonna give him an A-plus for "Love in Bloom."

WYKOWSKI  Jesus, you are a moron. Go look in the latrine and see where you dropped your brains.

SELRIDGE  I couldn't help it. I couldn't.

EUGENE  You win, Arnold. It's your money.

(EPSTEIN *starts for the money*)

WYKOWSKI  It never fails. It's always the Jews who end up with the money. Ain't that right, Roy?

SELRIDGE  Don't ask me. I never met a Jew before the army.

WYKOWSKI  They're easy to spot. (*To* EPSTEIN) There's one . . . (*To* EUGENE) . . . And there's another one. (*To all*) They're the ones who slide the bacon under their toast so no one sees them eat it. Ain't that right, Jerome?

EPSTEIN  (*Calmly*)  I'm tired of taking that Jew crap from you, Wykowski. I know you can probably beat the hell out of me, but I'm not going to take it from you anymore, understand?

39

WYKOWSKI   Sure you will. You'll take any shit from
me . . . Come on. Come on. Let's see how tough you
are. I'll knock the Alka-Seltzer right out of your
asshole.

HENNESEY   Cut it out, Kowski. What difference does
it make what religion he is?

WYKOWSKI   I didn't start it. Epstein's the one who
thinks he's too good to take orders, isn't he? Well,
I'm not doing a hundred push-ups for any goddamn
goof-up anymore. If he doesn't shape up, I'll bust his
face whether he's got a Jew nose or not.
   *(They both go for each other, but are restrained by the
   others)*

CARNEY   *(Seeing* TOOMEY *coming)*   Ten-HUT!
   *(Suddenly* SERGEANT TOOMEY *appears in his pants
   and an undershirt. All snap to attention)*

TOOMEY   What the hell is going on here?

HENNESEY   Nothing, Sergeant.

TOOMEY   What do you mean nothing? I heard threats,
challenges and an invitation to bust the nose of
members of minority races. Now are you still telling me that nothing was going on here?

HENNESEY   Yes, Sergeant.

TOOMEY   I think you'd better sleep on that answer,
boy. And to make sure you get a good night's sleep,
you get yourself good and tired with one hundred
push-ups. On the floor, dogface, and let me hear you
count. *(*HENNESEY *gets on the ground and immediately
starts to do push-ups)* If I hear any more racial slurs
from this platoon, some dumb bastard is going to be
shoveling cow shit with a teaspoon for a month.

Especially if I hear it from a Polack! LIGHTS OUT!!

*(The lights suddenly go out, leaving only a tiny spot on* EUGENE*)*

EUGENE *(To the audience)* ... I never liked Wykowski much and I didn't like him any better after tonight ... But the one I hated most was myself because I didn't stand up for Epstein, a fellow Jew. Maybe I was afraid of Wykowski or maybe it was because Epstein sort of sometimes asked for it, but since the guys didn't pick on me that much, I figured I'd just stay sort of neutral ... like Switzerland ... Then I wrote in my memoirs what every guy's last desire would be if he was killed in the war. I never intended to show it to anyone, but still I felt a little ashamed of betraying their secret and private thoughts ... Possibly the only one who felt worse than I did was Hennesey on the floor.

HENNESEY *(Doing push-ups)* ... forty-one ... forty-two ... forty-three ... forty-four ... forty-five.

*(It is weeks later, in a section of the latrine.* SELRIDGE *and* CARNEY *are finishing shaving.* HENNESEY *is brushing his hair. They are in their underwear, some with their trousers on)*

SELRIDGE Forty-eight-hour pass, hot damn! If I make it with one woman every four hours, that means I could have ... er ... I could have ... *(He thinks)*— a lot of women!

HENNESEY I'd be careful. You know what you could get.

SELRIDGE Yeah. Relief.

WYKOWSKI *(Comes in looking very angry)* Son of a bitch! goddamn son of a bitch!!

SELRIDGE  What's wrong?

WYKOWSKI *(Holds up the empty wallet)* Someone broke into my footlocker last night. They emptied my wallet. They took my pay and every cent I had in the world. Sixty-two bucks. Dirty bastard.

CARNEY  How do you know it was stolen? Maybe you lost it.

WYKOWSKI  I counted it before I hit the sack. I was saving it for the big weekend. Don't think I'm not wise to who did it. Maybe they both did it together.

HENNESEY  How do you know it was them? Maybe it was one of us.

WYKOWSKI  . . . Was it? Was it?

SELRIDGE  You think I'm crazy enough to tell you if I stole your money?

WYKOWSKI  It was Epstein, I'm telling you. He's trying to get back at me for what I said that night.

HENNESEY  Maybe he's sore at you but he's not the kind that steals money.

WYKOWSKI  Who asked you, Hennesey? What are you, one of those Irish Jews? All I did was call him a couple of names. Where I come from we're all po- lacks, dagos, niggers and sheenies. That stuff doesn't mean crap to me. You're a mick, what do I care?

HENNESEY  Half mick, half nigger.
     *(WYKOWSKI and SELRIDGE look at each other)*

WYKOWSKI  Are you serious?

HENNESEY  Yeah. My father's Irish, my mother's col- ored.

SELRIDGE  You can't be colored. They wouldn't let you in with us.

HENNESEY  I never told anybody.

WYKOWSKI  Yeah, but I guessed it. It was something I couldn't put my finger on but I knew something was wrong with you.

HENNESEY  I'm black Irish, that's as colored as I am. But now we know how you think, don't we, Kow-ski?

WYKOWSKI  I'm laying for you, Hennesey. After I get the bastard who stole my money, I'll settle my score with you.

CARNEY  Does Toomey know?

WYKOWSKI  I think so. He must have heard me. Some-body steals sixty-two bucks, people hear about it.
    (TOOMEY *appears*)

TOOMEY (*Calmly*)  Gentlemen, I think we have a prob-lem. All those wishing to help me solve it, get your asses in here before the firing squad leaves for the weekend. ON THE DOUBLE!!! Ten-hut!! (*The lights go up on the barracks area, off on the latrine. All six soldiers rush in and line up at attention in front of their bunks.* TOOMEY, *dressed for weekend leave, walks slowly in front of them, thinking very seriously*) . . . I've been in this man's army now for twelve years, four months and twenty-three days and during my ten-ure as a noncommissioned officer, I have put up with everything from mutiny to sodomy. I consider mutiny and sodomy relatively minor offenses. Mu-tiny is an act of aggression due to a rising expression of unreleased repressed feelings. Sodomy is the re-sult of doing something you don't want to do with someone you don't want to do it with because of no access to do what you want to do with someone you can't get to do it with.

EUGENE *(To the audience)* It makes sense if you think it out slowly.

TOOMEY Burglary, on the other hand, is a cheap shit crime. And I frown on that. In the past thirty-one days, you boys have made some fine progress. You're not fighting soldiers yet, but I'd match you up against some Nazi cocktail waitresses any time. That's why it was my recommendation that this platoon receive a forty-eight-hour pass ... But until we clear up the mystery of Private Wykowski's missing sixty-two dollars, there will be no forty-eight-hour passes issued until you are old and gray soldiers of World War Two, marching as American Legionnaires in the Armistice Day Parade. I am asking the guilty party to place sixty-two dollars on this here footlocker within the next thirty seconds ... I offer no leniency, no forgiveness and no abstention from punishment. What I do offer is honor and integrity, and the respect of his fellow soldiers, knowing that it was *his* act of courage that enabled them to enjoy the brief freedom they so richly deserve. *(He looks at his watch)* I am counting down to thirty ... It is of this time that heroes are made. One ... two ... three ... four ... five ... *(They all look at each other silently)* six seven ... eight ...
   *(Suddenly EPSTEIN takes out his wallet, removes some bills, counts off sixty-two dollars and puts it on the footlocker in front of him. The others look silently ahead)*

EPSTEIN   There's sixty-two dollars, if anyone cares to count it.

TOOMEY   I don't think that will be necessary, Private Epstein . . . Wykowski, pick up your money. (WYKOWSKI *picks it up and starts to count*) I SAID DON'T COUNT IT, BOY!!!! (WYKOWSKI *stops, folds it and puts it in his pocket and returns to attention*) Private Epstein, do you have anything to say?

EPSTEIN   No, Sergeant.

TOOMEY   May I ask why you decided to return the money?

EPSTEIN   I chose to.

TOOMEY   You chose to. Knowing full well that swift and just punishment may be inflicted upon you when and if this is reported to the Commanding Officer?

EPSTEIN   I know it only too well.

TOOMEY   You could have kept quiet about this incident. Chances are no one would have found out or been the wiser.

EPSTEIN   I didn't see any reason why five innocent men should suffer a loss of privilege because of one guilty one.

TOOMEY   Private Wykowski . . . Is it your wish that I report this incident and the guilty party to the Commanding Officer?

WYKOWSKI   I just want my money, Sergeant. I can deal with the bastard who took it on my own.
   (TOOMEY *stares at him, then reaches into his pocket and takes out some folded bills*)

45

TOOMEY    Last night at 0100 hours I wandered through this barracks and saw carelessness and complacency. Wykowski's wallet was lying in an open footlocker inviting weakness, avarice and temptation. *I took your sixty-two dollars, Wykowski, and returned the empty wallet in its place. I did it to teach you a lesson . . . Instead, I got . . . submarined. (He goes nose to nose with* EPSTEIN) Private Epstein, are you such a goddamn ignorant fool to take the blame for something you were completely innocent of?

EPSTEIN    The army has its logic, I have my own.

TOOMEY    The army's "logic," as you call it, is to instill discipline, obedience and unquestioned faith in superiors. What the hell is yours?

EPSTEIN    Since I'm not guilty of a crime, I reserve the privilege to keep my own motives a matter of confidentiality.

TOOMEY    That's where you're wrong, soldier. Confessing to a crime you didn't commit is no less an offense to *not* confessing to one you *did* commit. That is called obstruction of justice. You may not like our rules, boy, but by God, you're going to clean every toilet and pisspot until you learn them. Confined to barracks until further notice. The rest of you are on forty-eight hours' leave. Fall out! . . . Epstein, I would like a word with you in private. *(The others break up and move to their bunks to discuss the event.* EPSTEIN *follows* TOOMEY *to the latrine.* TOOMEY *turns, faces* EPSTEIN, *lowers his voice)* Listen to me, you flyspeck on a mound of horse shit. You're taking me on, ain't you? Well, you're making a big mistake because I have a nutcracker that crunches the testicles of men who take me on . . . How the hell do you think you can beat me?

EPSTEIN  I'm not trying to beat you, Sergeant. I'm trying to work with you.

TOOMEY  (*Looks at him sideways*)  I think you're low on batteries, Epstein. I think some plumber turned off your fountain of knowledge. What the hell do you mean, *working* with me?

EPSTEIN  I don't think it's necessary to dehumanize a man to get him to perform. You can get better results raising our spirits than lowering our dignity.

TOOMEY  Why in the hell did you put back money you knew you didn't take?

EPSTEIN  Because I knew that *you* did. I saw you take it. I think inventing a crime that didn't exist to enforce your theories of discipline is Neanderthal in its conception.

TOOMEY  (*Gets closer*)  I can arrange it, Epstein, that from now on you get nothing to eat in the mess hall except cotton balls. You ever eat cotton balls, Epstein? You can chew it till 1986, it don't swallow . . . Men do not face enemy machine guns because they have been treated with kindness. They face them because they have a bayonet up their ass. I don't *want* them human. I want them obedient.

EPSTEIN  Egyptian Kings made their slaves obedient. Eventually they lost their slaves *and* their kingdom.

TOOMEY  Yeah, well, I may lose mine but before you go, you're going to build me the biggest goddamn pyramid you ever saw . . . I'm trying to save these

47

boys' lives, you crawling bookworm. Stand in my way and I'll pulverize you into chicken droppings.

EPSTEIN  It should be an interesting contest, Sergeant.

TOOMEY  After I crush your testicles, you can replace them with the cotton balls. *(He glares at* EPSTEIN, *then exits quickly)* . . . Neanderthal in its conception, Jesus Christ!

CARNEY *(Tying his tie)*  So who really stole the money?

SELRIDGE *(Brushing his shoes)*  Toomey stole Wykowski's sixty-two bucks but Epstein stole Toomey's *idea* of stealing Wykowski's sixty-two bucks.

HENNESEY  Why?

SELRIDGE  Did you ever see a big fat walrus screw another big fat walrus? There's no point to it but they do it anyway . . . You comin', Kows?

WYKOWSKI  In a minute.

CARNEY  I'll tell you something. The army is really dumb. If the navy is this dumb, we're gonna have to take a train to Europe.

    *(CARNEY and HENNESEY leave. EPSTEIN returns to the room)*

WYKOWSKI  I don't get you, Epstein. What'd you do a dumb-ass thing like that for?

EPSTEIN  You wouldn't understand.

WYKOWSKI  Why not? Am I too dumb? Dumb polack is that what I am? Now who's calling who names?

EPSTEIN  You are. If no one confessed, no one goes on leave. If any of the other guys really did it, I'd end up cleaning the toilet bowls anyway. He's trying to break my spirit.

WYKOWSKI  How'd you figure that out?

EPSTEIN  Talmudic reasoning.

WYKOWSKI  What?

EPSTEIN  Talmudic. You weigh both sides of an issue, then choose the one that's the most interesting. Unless, of course, the other guy picks that one first.

WYKOWSKI  Yeah? Well, whatever . . . Anyway, I owe you one. You stuck your neck out for us. *(He extends his hand)* I like to pay back my debts.

EPSTEIN  *(Looks at the extended hand)*  You really want to shake my hand, Wykowski?

WYKOWSKI  Listen, it's not going to come out again, so take your chance while you got it.

EPSTEIN  Let's not be hypocritical. I did what I did for me, not for you.

WYKOWSKI  *(Smiles)*  I'm not going to make any more Jew cracks at you, Epstein. 'Cause you're a shitheel no matter what you are.
    *(He goes. The others go off.* EUGENE *sits on his bed, smiles and shakes his head at* EPSTEIN*)*

EUGENE  Why do you always have to do things the hard way?

EPSTEIN  It makes life more interesting.

EUGENE  It also makes a lot of problems.

EPSTEIN  Without problems, the day would be over at eleven o'clock in the morning.
    *(*EPSTEIN *starts to change into fatigues)*

EUGENE  I admire what you did back there, Arnold. You remind me of my brother, sometimes. He was always standing up for his principles too.

EPSTEIN  Principles are okay. But sometimes they get in the way of reason.

EUGENE  Then how do you know which one is the right one?

EPSTEIN  You have to get involved. You don't get involved enough, Eugene.

EUGENE  What do you mean?

EPSTEIN  You're a witness. You're always standing around *watching* what's happening. Scribbling in your book what other people do. You have to get in the middle of it. You have to take sides. Make a contribution to the fight.

EUGENE  What fight?

EPSTEIN  *Any* fight. The one you believe in.

EUGENE  Yeah. I know what you mean. Sometimes I feel like I'm invisible. Like The Shadow. I can see everyone else but they can't see me. That's what I think writers are. Sort of invisible.

EPSTEIN  Not Tolstoy. Not Dostoyevsky. Not Herman Melville.

EUGENE  Yeah. I have to read those guys.

TOOMEY *(Offstage)*  EPSTEIN! I DON'T HEAR NO GODDAMN FLUSHING!!

EPSTEIN  I'd better go. I have to get involved with toilet bowls.

EUGENE  I'd love to talk to you more, Arnold.

EPSTEIN  I'm available.

EUGENE  Well, maybe when I get back Sunday night.

EPSTEIN  Sure. Anytime you want . . . Just make sure you don't come back pregnant.

EUGENE   Are you kidding? I'm wearing three pairs of socks.

EPSTEIN   Make sure you put them on the right place.
   *(He leaves)*

EUGENE *(To the audience)*   Soo—I was off to Biloxi to live out my fantasies. Love or sex, I'd settle for either one . . . I put powder and Aqua Velva in and under every conceivable part of my body.
   *(CARNEY comes back in)*

CARNEY   I've been waiting for you.

EUGENE   Okay. Let's go!

CARNEY   Wait—wait! I need a favor from you.

EUGENE   What is it?

CARNEY   Sit down. I need your opinion. And please, tell me the truth. *(EUGENE waits, CARNEY lowers his head and begins to sing "Embraceable You." The curtain starts to descend as EUGENE looks helplessly at the audience)*

*Curtain*

# ACT TWO

*A section of a small, tacky room in a cheap hotel. There are two worn armchairs at angle to each other. Seated are EU-GENE and CARNEY. SELRIDGE paces impatiently. All three are smoking cigarettes, puffing away nervously.*

SELRIDGE *(Looking at his watch)* Almost a half-hour he's been in there. It doesn't take a half-hour. She couldn't make any money that way.

CARNEY Maybe he went twice. Or three times.

SELRIDGE Wykowski could keep going for six months straight. That's not the point. They charge you every time, that's the point.

CARNEY Maybe she gave him a free one because of his unusual condition.

EUGENE You mean she charges you every time you have a—

SELRIDGE *(Pacing)* That's right.

EUGENE How does she know when you have one?

SELRIDGE *(Stops and looks at him)* Because your eyes spin around and when they stop on two pineapples, you just had one. *(To CARNEY)* Is this guy for real?

CARNEY And he's from New York City too. Can you believe it?

EUGENE *(Defensively)* I make out on my own. I just never go to places like this . . . And you mean, if you have a—a thing more than once, she keeps count?

CARNEY Yeah. Actually, every time you do it, she makes an X on your head with her lipstick.
*(He blows smoke in EUGENE's face)*

EUGENE Hey, don't blow smoke in my face. I'll stink up from tobacco.

55

CARNEY   Stop worrying. Nothing can penetrate your Aqua Velva . . . If you don't like it, what are you smoking for?

EUGENE *(Looks at the cigarette in his hand)*   I didn't know I was. Somebody must have handed it to me. *(He puts it out hard in the ashtray. He gets up and paces. To* SELRIDGE*)* You want to sit down?

SELRIDGE   And break my concentration? *(He looks at his watch)* Hurry up, dammit, I'm going to pass my peak.

EUGENE   What if she's ugly? I mean really ugly.

SELRIDGE   . . . Close your eyes and think of some girl in high school.

EUGENE   I don't want to close my eyes. That's the same as doing it to yourself.

SELRIDGE   Not if you're feeling somebody underneath you . . . Or on top of you.

EUGENE *(Stops)*   What do you mean, on *top* of you. Who would be on top of me?

SELRIDGE   She would. She could be anywhere. Under a table. On a chair or an ironing board.

EUGENE   *An ironing board???* What kind of girl is this? I thought we were going just to a regular place.

SELRIDGE   I didn't mention anything that wasn't regular. I mean don't you know anything? Do you have any idea of how many possible positions there are?

EUGENE   Yeah. Sure. I'm not an ignoramus.

CARNEY *(To* EUGENE*)*   How many positions are there?

EUGENE *(Looks at* CARNEY, *then points to* SELRIDGE*)*   I'm having this conversation with him.

SELRIDGE   Okay. How many positions are there?

EUGENE *(Thinks)* . . . American or Worldwide?

SELRIDGE *(Laughs)* You don't know shit, Jerome.

EUGENE   Maybe not actual experience. But I have all the information I need.

SELRIDGE   Then how many positions are there, in this galaxy?

EUGENE   For how much?

SELRIDGE   Loser pays for the bang.

EUGENE   Don't call it a bang. I'm here for pleasure, not to get banged.

CARNEY *(Laughs)* This guy's a riot.

SELRIDGE   For five bucks. How many positions are there?

EUGENE   I'm thinking. Give me a minute.

SELRIDGE   You want me to tell you?

EUGENE   No.

SELRIDGE   Well, I'll tell you. Seventeen.

EUGENE   How do you know?

SELRIDGE   Because I've tried them all.

EUGENE   You're wrong. There's at least *fifty-two* different positions.

SELRIDGE   *Fifty-two??* . . . You're crazy! . . . Where'd you get that from?

EUGENE   I saw a dirty deck of cards once.

SELRIDGE *(To* CARNEY*)* This guy's worse than Epstein.

EUGENE   You owe me five bucks.

SELRIDGE   Listen, twerp. You're lucky if you do *one* position.

EUGENE   I'm not going to do *anything* if it's on an ironing board.

CARNEY   Why not? You'll get your shirt pressed for free.

SELRIDGE   *(Looks at his watch)*   Thirty-four minutes. Damn Wykowski! We should have let the normal guys go first.

EUGENE   *(To the audience)*   I didn't want my first time to be like this . . . I really tried to meet somebody nice but there are twenty-one thousand soldiers on leave in Biloxi and fourteen girls . . . Those are tough odds. Especially since the fourteen girls all go to Catholic school and are handcuffed to nuns.
   *(WYKOWSKI appears with a know-it-all look on his face. He straightens his tie as he chews gum)*

SELRIDGE   Well??? . . . Tell us!

WYKOWSKI   She wants to see me again after the war.
   *(He puts on his cap and disappears)*

SELRIDGE   *(Looks around)*   Okay, whose turn is it?

EUGENE   You go ahead. I just had lunch. I don't want to get cramps.
   *(CARNEY nods assent)*

SELRIDGE   *(Straightens himself up)*   I'll try to leave a little something for you guys. *(He disappears)* Hey! How are you?

CARNEY   *(Looks at EUGENE)*   We don't have to do this, you know. There's a dance over at the U.S.O.

EUGENE  This isn't your first time, is it? I mean, you've done it before, haven't you?

CARNEY  Oh, yeah. Sure. Are you kidding? . . . Not a lot. About five or six times.

EUGENE  So why are you doing it again?

CARNEY  You're not through after five or six times. If you live long enough, you've got twelve thousand more left.

EUGENE  I don't know why I'm so scared. I'm never going to see her again. I just don't want to seem foolish. I think I'm afraid she's going to laugh at me.

CARNEY  Not if she gets paid. If she laughed at you, you would be entitled to a refund.
(SELRIDGE *comes out, buttoning his shirt*)

EUGENE  You're through already? That was fast.

SELRIDGE  (*Unhappy*)  I didn't make it to the bed. I knew I hit my peak too soon.
(*And he is gone*)

CARNEY  (*Looks at* EUGENE)  Listen, I think I'm gonna go to the dance.

EUGENE  How come?

CARNEY  I said before I did it five or six times but it was all with the same girl. We're sort of engaged. She might not like it.

EUGENE  I bet she wouldn't. I didn't know you had a girl. That's terrific. What's her name?

CARNEY  Charlene.

EUGENE  Charlene! Wow! Sounds sexy. You think you'll get married?

CARNEY   Well, it's a fifty-fifty chance. She's got another boyfriend in Albany . . . So what are you going to do?

EUGENE   Well, the thing is, I don't have a girl. I've got to learn on my own. Epstein says I have to get more involved in life. I think I'm in the perfect place for an involvement.

CARNEY   Okay. Maybe I'll see you later. *(He puts on his cap)* Listen. Don't expect too much the first time. What I mean is, if it doesn't go all that terrific, don't give up on it for good.

EUGENE   I'm not a quitter. I'm dedicating my life to getting it right.

CARNEY   You putting this in your memoirs?

EUGENE   Sure. I put everything in my memoirs.

CARNEY   That's smart. Because people don't like books unless there's sex in them . . . Good luck, kid. *(He takes a photo of* EUGENE *with his hand on the door)*

EUGENE *(To the audience)*   . . . And thus, the young man they called Eugene bade farewell to his youth, turned and entered the Temple of Fire.
*(The scenery changes to* ROWENA'*s room.* EUGENE *is hidden behind a screen.* ROWENA *is sitting at her vanity, smoking and trying to be patient)*

ROWENA *(Calls out)*   How you doing, honey?

EUGENE *(From behind the screen)*   Okay.

ROWENA   You having any trouble in there?

EUGENE   No. No trouble.

ROWENA   What the hell you doing for ten minutes? C'mon, kid. I haven't got all day. *(*EUGENE *appears. He* *is wearing his khaki shorts, shoes and socks. A cigarette dangles from his lips.* ROWENA *looks at him)* Listen. You can keep your shorts on if you want but I have a rule against wearing army shoes in bed.

EUGENE *(Looks down)* Oh. I'm sorry. I just forgot to take them off. *(He sits on the bed and very slowly starts to unlace them. To the audience)* I started to sweat like crazy. I prayed my Aqua Velva was working.

(ROWENA *sprays around her with perfume from her atomizer)*

ROWENA You don't mind a little perfume, do you, honey? The boy before you had on a gallon of Aqua Velva.

EUGENE *(Looks at the audience, then at her)* No, I don't mind. You can spray some on me. *(She smiles and sprays him playfully)* Gee, it smells good.

ROWENA If you'd like a bottle for your girl friend, I sell them. Five dollars apiece.

EUGENE You sell perfume too?

ROWENA I sell hard-to-get items. Silk stockings. Black panties . . . You interested?

EUGENE *(Earnestly)* Do you carry men's clothing?

ROWENA *(Laughs)* That's cute. You're cute, honey . . . You want me to take your shoes off?

EUGENE I can do it. Honest. I can do it.
(*He gets his first shoe off)*

ROWENA Is this your first time?

EUGENE My first time? *(He laughs)* Are you kidding? That's funny . . . Noo . . . It's my second time . . . The first time they were closed.

ROWENA  You don't smoke cigarettes either, do you? *(She takes the cigarette out of* EUGENE's *mouth)*

EUGENE  How'd you know?

ROWENA  You looked like your face was on fire . . . If you want to look older, why don't you try a mustache?

EUGENE  I did but it wouldn't grow in on the left side . . . What's your name?

ROWENA  Rowena . . . What's yours?

EUGENE  My name? *(To the audience)* I suddenly panicked. Supposing this girl kept a diary.

ROWENA  Well?

EUGENE *(Quickly)*  Jack . . . Er . . . Jack Mulgroovey.

ROWENA  Yeah? I knew a *Tom* Mulgreevy once.

EUGENE  No. Mine is Mulgroovey. Oo not ee.

ROWENA  Where you from, Jack?

EUGENE *(With a slight accent)*  Texarkana.

ROWENA  Is that right?

EUGENE  Yes, ma'am.

ROWENA  Is that Texas or Arkansas?

EUGENE  Arkansas, I think.

ROWENA  You *think*?

EUGENE  I left there when I was two. Then we moved to Georgia.

ROWENA  Really? You a cracker?

EUGENE  What's a cracker?

ROWENA  Someone from Georgia.

EUGENE  Oh, yeah. I'm a cracker. The whole family's crackers . . . Were you born in Biloxi?

ROWENA    No. Gulfport. I still live there with my husband.

EUGENE    Your husband??... You're married??... My God! If he finds me here he'll kill me.

ROWENA    No he won't.

EUGENE    Does he know that you're a—you're a—

ROWENA    Sure he does. That's how we met. He's in the Navy. He was one of my best customers. He still is.

EUGENE    You mean you *charge* your own husband??

ROWENA    I mean he's my best lover... You gonna do it from there, cowboy? 'Cause I'll have to make some adjustments.

EUGENE    I'm ready. (*To* ROWENA) Here I come.
(*She holds the open blanket. He gets into the bed and clings to the side*)

ROWENA    If you're gonna hang on the edge like that, we're gonna be on the floor in two minutes.

EUGENE    I didn't want to crowd you.

ROWENA    Crowding is what this is all about, Tex. (*She pulls him over. He kneels above her*)    Okay, honey. Do your stuff.

EUGENE    What stuff is that?

ROWENA    Whatever you like to do.

EUGENE    Why don't you start and I'll catch up.

ROWENA    Didn't anyone ever tell you what to do?

EUGENE    My brother once showed me but you look a lot different than my brother.

ROWENA  You're sweet. I went to high school with a boy like you. I had the biggest damn crush on him.

EUGENE *(He is still above her)*  Do you have a hanky?

ROWENA  Anything wrong?

EUGENE  My nose is running.
*(She takes the hanky and wipes his nose)*

ROWENA  Better?

EUGENE  Thank you. Listen, please don't be offended but I really don't care if this is a wonderful experience or not. I just want to get it over with.

ROWENA  Whatever you say . . . Lights on or off?

EUGENE  Actually I'd like a blindfold. *(She reaches over and turns off the lamp)* . . . Oh, God . . . Oh, MY GOD!!! *(He slumps down)* . . . WOW! . . . I DID IT! . . . I DID IT!!

ROWENA  Anything else, honey?

EUGENE *(Calmer, more mature)*  Yes. I'd like two bottles of perfume and a pair of black panties.
*Blackout*

*(Lights up on a section of the barracks. It's late Sunday night. SELRIDGE, CARNEY and EPSTEIN are lying on their bunks. WYKOWSKI, pacing, has EUGENE's notebook of memoirs. CARNEY is on his stomach reading a letter and EPSTEIN is reading a worn paperback of Kafka)*

WYKOWSKI  . . . I can't believe what this creep's been writing about us . . . Listen to this . . . "No matter how lunatic I think Sergeant Toomey is, there is method in his madness. He is winning the game.

Each day we drop a little of our own personalities and become more obedient, more robot-like, until what was once an intelligent, thinking human being is now nothing but a khaki idiot. Yesterday, in front of everybody, he made Epstein unscrew the top of his head and take his brains out."

EPSTEIN *(Without looking up from his book)* I fooled him. I only took out my mucous membranes.

WYKOWSKI *(Continues reading)* . . . "I am fighting hard to retain my identity, and the only time I am able to hold on to who I am is in the still, still of the night."
*(HENNESEY comes in from outside)*

HENNESEY Wow, what a weekend. How'd you guys do?

WYKOWSKI Hey, Hennesey. You ought to listen to this. You're in this too.

HENNESEY What is it?
*(He starts loosening his tie)*

WYKOWSKI *The Secret and Private Memoirs of Eugene M. Jerome.*

HENNESEY He let you read it?

WYKOWSKI No, but we're going to ask him if it's all right when we get through.
*(He and SELRIDGE laugh)*

HENNESEY You have no right to read that. That's like opening someone's mail.

WYKOWSKI Bullshit. It's all about us. Private things about every one of us. That's public domain like in the newspapers.

EPSTEIN *(Without looking up from his book)* A newspaper is published. Unpublished memoirs are the sole and private property of the writer.

WYKOWSKI I thought all Jews were doctors. I didn't know they were lawyers too.

EPSTEIN I'm not a Jew anymore, Wykowski.

WYKOWSKI What do you mean?

EPSTEIN I converted to Catholicism yesterday. In six weeks I hope to become a priest and my first act of service to the Holy Father is to have you excommunicated, so get off my ass.

SELRIDGE *(Laughs)* That's good. That's funny. goddamn Jews are really funny. Hey, Epstein, I'm beginning to like you, I swear to Christ.

WYKOWSKI *(Annoyed)* You guys interested in hearing the rest of this or not?

HENNESEY No, I'm not. *(He starts toward the latrine, stops)* I thought you were Gene's friend, Epstein.

EPSTEIN He didn't lock his locker. Why then would he leave something so private in an open locker? There's no logic to it. I have no interest in illogical things.

HENNESEY *(To EPSTEIN)* You tell Gene I had nothing to do with this. You hear me?
*(And he is off to the latrine)*

SELRIDGE Go on. After ". . . still, still of the night."

WYKOWSKI *(Reading)* . . . "At night I listen to the others breathing in their sleep and it's then that their fears and self-doubts become even more apparent than during their waking hours . . . One night a sudden scream from Selridge that sounded like he was calling out the name Louise. Is Louise his girl or possibly his mother?"

SELRIDGE   He's full of crap.

WYKOWSKI   Who's Louise?

SELRIDGE   My mother. But he's full of crap. I never called my mother Louise.

WYKOWSKI   Poor baby, wants his mother.
*(He continues reading)*

CARNEY   I don't want to hear any more of this. I don't like being spied on.

WYKOWSKI   *(Looks at the book)*   Dirty bastard! Wait'll you hear what he writes about me.
*(Suddenly* EUGENE *appears, coming back from town)*

SELRIDGE   It's him. Put it away.
*(*WYKOWSKI *slips the book under his bunk, pretends to play cards with* SELRIDGE. EUGENE *enters with a big, self-satisfied smile on his face and a very "cocky" walk)*

EUGENE   Hi, guys! *(They all look up, mutter their hellos and resume their activities.* EUGENE *waits expectantly for someone to ask about his adventure but no one does)* So how was your weekend?

CARNEY   Fine.

WYKOWSKI   Great.

SELRIDGE   The best.

EUGENE   Good—good—good—good—good.

CARNEY *(To* EUGENE*)*   Well?

EUGENE   Well what?

CARNEY   What was it like? Give us details . . . Was it "Empty Saddles in the Old Corral" or was it "Swing Swing Swing"?

EUGENE   It was sort of—"Moonlight Cocktails" . . . It was chatty.

WYKOWSKI   Chatty?? Your first time in the sack with a pro was "chatty"?

EUGENE   She's not a pro. She only does it on weekends.

WYKOWSKI   So what does that make her? A semi-pro?

SELRIDGE *(Laughs)*   Great! That was great. Perfect remark, Kows . . .

EUGENE   At least we talked to each other. I wasn't in and out of there in two seconds. She was a person to me, not a pro.

EPSTEIN *(Still reading his book)*   Self-righteous, Eugene. Be on guard against self-righteousness.

EUGENE *(Unties his tie, starts to unbutton his shirt)*   . . . The second time was "Swing Swing Swing."
*(He smiles)*

SELRIDGE   The *second* time? You paid twice?

EUGENE   No. It was a "freebie." On the house.

WYKOWSKI   You're full of it.

CARNEY   Why would she give you a free one?

EUGENE   Maybe I was her one millionth customer.
*(He chuckles at his joke)*

WYKOWSKI   Hey, Jerome. Blow it out your barracks bag.
*(EUGENE doesn't find what he's looking for. He seems*

*disturbed. He looks through his locker, under his bunk and mattress)*

EUGENE    Has anyone seen my notebook?

WYKOWSKI *(Very deliberate)*    What notebook is that?

EUGENE    The one I'm always writing in . . . Arnold, did you see it?

EPSTEIN    Why did you leave your locker unlocked?

EUGENE    Because I lost my key in the shower drain. There was nothing valuable in there except my book. I thought I could trust people around here.

WYKOWSKI    That's really funny, Jerome, 'cause we thought we could trust you too.

EUGENE    What does that mean?
        (WYKOWSKI *reaches under his bunk and takes out the notebook. He opens it up and* EUGENE *makes a move toward it but* WYKOWSKI *jumps on top of his bunk and extends his foot to ward off* EUGENE. *He starts to read)*

WYKOWSKI    "One night a sudden scream from Selridge that sounded like he was calling out the name Louise. Is Louise his girl or possibly his mother?"

EUGENE *(Furiously)*    You had no right to read that. Give it to me, Kowski.

CARNEY    Give it to him. Nobody's interested.

WYKOWSKI    No? You interested in what he thinks about you, Donny baby?

EUGENE *(Lunges for him)*    Give it to me, goddammit!!
        (SELRIDGE *reaches quickly and grabs* EUGENE's *arm and bends it behind his back.* EUGENE *knows one move and it's broken)*

SELRIDGE  I'm just gonna hold your arm. If you want it broken, it's up to you.

CARNEY  What does he say about me?

EUGENE  Kowski, please don't read it.

WYKOWSKI  If it gets boring, I'll stop. *(He reads)* "I can't make Don Carney out yet. Basically I like him and we've had some interesting talks, if you don't mind sticking to popular music and baseball. But there's something about him you can't count on and if I was ever in real trouble, Don Carney's the last one I'd turn to."
> (CARNEY *and* EUGENE *look at each other. The others are quiet)*

CARNEY  Well, let's just hope you never have to count on me.
> *(He is hurt. He gets up, walks to the side and lights up a cigarette)*

EUGENE  *(To* CARNEY*)*  It doesn't mean anything. It's just the thoughts in my head when I'm writing it. They change every day.

HENNESEY  Let him go, Selridge.

SELRIDGE  You want to take his place? I don't care whose arm I break.

WYKOWSKI  Okay, you ready for the best part? Here's the best part: "Wykowski is pure animal. His basic instincts are all physical and he eats his meals like a horse eating his oats." Hey, Epstein! Can I sue him for defamation of—what is it?

EPSTEIN  Character. Only if his intent is to prove malice and in your case it's not possible.

SELRIDGE  Go on. What else does he say about you?

WYKOWSKI *(Reads on)* "He masturbates in bed four or five times a night. He has no shame about it and his capacities are inexhaustible. Sometimes when he has a discharge, he announces it to the room. 'Number five torpedo fired! Loading number six!'" *(To the others)* That's really good reporting. This guy should be on *Time* magazine or something.

EUGENE *(Near tears)* Please stop it. You want to read it, read it to yourself.

WYKOWSKI What do you mean? You're making me famous. Maybe the movies'll buy this. Great picture for John Wayne.

SELRIDGE Is there any more?

WYKOWSKI Yeah. Where was I?

SELRIDGE You just fired number five.

WYKOWSKI Oh yeah. Here. *(He reads)* "Despite Wykowski's lack of culture, sensitivity or the pursuit of anything minutely intellectual, his greatest strength is his consistency of character and his earnest belief that he belongs on the battlefield. He is clearly the best soldier in the platoon, dependable under pressure and it would not surprise me if Wykowski came out of this war with the Medal of Honor." *(He looks at* EUGENE*)* . . . You really mean that, Jerome?

EUGENE I told you, I don't mean any of it. I get a thought and I write it down. Right now I would describe you in three words. "A yellow bastard!"

WYKOWSKI They don't give the Medal of Honor to yellow bastards . . . Let him go, Sel. (SELRIDGE *lets him go.* EUGENE *rubs his arm in pain)* . . . Why do you want

71

to write this stuff down for? You're just gonna make a lot of guys unhappy.

EUGENE    What I write is *my* business. Give me my book.

    *(He reaches for it)*

EPSTEIN    Wait a minute. *(As* WYKOWSKI *extends the book,* EPSTEIN *snatches it from his hand)* I think I deserve to hear *my* life story.

EUGENE    Arnold, I beg you. Don't read it. They're my private thoughts and if you take them, you steal from me.

EPSTEIN    I gather then it's unflattering. Don't you know me by now, Gene? I can't be unflattered. I'm past it . . . However, if you don't want me to read it, I won't read it. But I don't think we'll be able to be truly honest with each other from this moment on.

EUGENE    *(Looks at* EPSTEIN*)*  . . . Put it back when you're through.

    *(He gets up and walks out of the room.* EPSTEIN *opens the book and starts to read to himself)*

WYKOWSKI    Don't we get to hear it?

EPSTEIN    Sure, Kowski. This is what we're fighting the war about, isn't it? *(He reads)* "Arnold Epstein is truly the most complex and fascinating man I've ever met and his constant and relentless pursuit of truth, logic and reason fascinates me in the same proportion as his obstinacy and unnecessary heroics drive me to distraction. But I love him for it. In the same manner that I love Joe DiMaggio for making the gesture of catching a long fly ball to center seem like the last miracle performed by God in modern times. But often I hold back showing my love and affection for Arnold because I think he might misinterpret it. It just happens to be my instinctive feeling—that Arnold is homosexual, and it bothers me that it bothers me." *(He closes the book. He looks at the others, who are all staring at him)* . . . Do you see why I find life so interesting? Here is a man of my own faith and background, potentially intelligent and talented, who in six weeks has come to the brilliant conclusion that a cretin like Wykowski is going to win the Medal of Honor and that I, his most esteemed and dearest friend, am a fairy. *(He tosses the book on EUGENE's bunk)* This is a problem worthy of a Talmudic scholar. Goodnight, fellas . . . It is my opinion that no one gets a wink of sleep tonight.

> *(Light up on the steps outside the barracks. A bare light bulb hangs above. EUGENE sits on the steps, smoking a cigarette and looking in the depths of despair.*
>
> *After a few moments, DON CARNEY comes out, leans against the post and lights up a cigarette)*

CARNEY  . . . Did she really give you a second one for free?
*(There is a moment's silence)*

EUGENE  Listen, I'm sorry about what I wrote in the book. I didn't mean it the way it sounded.

CARNEY  Forget about it. You don't really know me anyway.

EUGENE  No. I suppose I don't.

CARNEY  . . . Is that what you think? That I'm someone who can't be counted on?

73

EUGENE  I don't know. You're just somebody who can never make up his mind. You say, "Let's go eat Chinese food." We walk in and order and then you say, "No, let's go get some burgers" . . . We play basketball and you never take a shot. You always pass off to somebody.

CARNEY  Because I'm not a good shooter.

EUGENE  You're as good as the rest of us. You just think about it too long. Then it's too late to take the shot . . .

CARNEY  And that's why I can't be counted on?

EUGENE  I wasn't writing about peacetime. I'm sure you're very dependable in peacetime. But we're at war. We're going to be fighting for our lives soon. I mean, somebody throws a grenade into your fox-hole, you don't want some guy staring at it for ten minutes saying, "What do you think we ought to do about it?"

CARNEY  Yeah, I can see that.

EUGENE  But you're still sore at me, aren't you?

CARNEY  I don't know. I have to think about it.

EUGENE  I figured you did.

CARNEY  . . . You know what Charlene once said to me? She said the reason she was seeing this other guy in Albany was because she didn't think I was someone she could count on.

EUGENE  You're kidding? Those exact words?

CARNEY  You think I'd ever forget them? She said she really liked me more than him but she wasn't sure I'd ever make up my mind. She didn't want to wait for me forever. So while she's waiting, she sees this guy up in Albany.

EUGENE   You see? That's what I meant.

CARNEY   Except for one thing. I'm not going to be in a foxhole with her with some Jap throwing in a grenade. I *have* to think about this because getting married is more serious.

EUGENE   More serious than being blown up?

CARNEY   Sure. Because if the grenade goes off, it's all over. Two seconds and you're gone. But if you make a mistake in marriage, you've got fifty years of misery. See what I mean?

EUGENE   Yeah. I see. *(He gets up and yawns)* Well, I'm tired. I'm going to turn in. How about you?

CARNEY   I don't know. Maybe.
(EUGENE *looks at the audience and nods as if to say,* "Didn't I tell you?" *He starts off*)

EUGENE   G'night.

CARNEY   G'night.
(EUGENE *goes inside.* CARNEY *sings a chorus of "That Old Feeling," during which time the scenery changes so that by the end of the song he is inside sitting on his bunk. The others wake up, angry.* CARNEY *retreats and lies down.*
*Moonlight is coming in through the barracks window. Suddenly the lights switch on. All six men are in their underwear, in their bunks.* TOOMEY *bangs loudly on the bedpost with his clipboard)*

TOOMEY   UP! Everybody UP!! goddammit!!! It is two-fifteen in the morning and I've got a headache, a problem and a goddamn temper all at the same time.

75

Move your asses, we've got some serious talking to do. MOVE IT! *(He bangs the bedpost again. They all get out of bed, mumbling their surprise and indignation. All stand at attention beside their bunks.* TOOMEY *paces back and forth, silently and angrily)* . . . Is there any among you who does not know the meaning of the word "fellatio"? *(Some of them look at each other)* For the uninformed, fellatio is the act of committing oral intercourse . . . Is there any among you who does not know the meaning of the word "oral" or "intercourse"? . . . It is encouraging to know that my platoon is made up of mental giants. At exactly 0155 this morning, Sergeant Riley of Baker Company entered the darkened latrine situated in his barracks . . . When he hit the light switch, lo and behold, he encountered two members of this regiment in the act of the aforementioned exercise . . . When I was in the Boy Scouts, that kind of thing came under the heading of "experimentation." In the wartime U.S. Army, it is considered a criminal offense, punishable by court-martial, dishonorable discharge and a possible five-year prison term . . . The soldier in Company B was a *(He looks at his clipboard)*—Private Harvey J. Lindstrom. The other soldier, whose back was to Sergeant Riley, was not seen and made his escape by jumping out an open window with his pants somewhere around his ankles, a feat of dexterity worthy of a paratrooper . . . Sergeant Riley, a man with five pounds of shrapnel in his right leg, gave chase to no avail but reported seeing the man enter this barracks at approximately oh two hundred hours . . . These are the facts, gentlemen. I will be brief. Does the guilty party wish to step forward, admit his indiscretion and save this company, what I promise you, will be pain, anguish and humiliation beyond the endurance of man. *(No one moves)* No, I didn't think so . . . I'm just going to have to pick him out, won't I? It's amazing what you can find out when you go eyeball to eyeball . . . *(He walks over to* WYKOWSKI *and indeed goes eyeball to eyeball. He moves on and does it with all six men)* Don't blink, Selridge . . . Look at me . . . Stand up, soldier . . . *(No one breathes. No one bats an eye)* There were two eyeballs in there whose shoes I wouldn't want to be in . . . Private Lindstrom will be interrogated in the morning. If he names the man he consorted with tonight, it is very possible Private Lindstrom's sentence will be significantly lessened. A worrisome thought to the gentleman whose eyeballs I just referred to . . . In the meantime all privileges on base are canceled, all weekend leaves are likewise canceled . . . The moral of this story is—when you get real horny, do unto yourself what you would otherwise do unto others . . .

> *(He turns and leaves. The others breathe at last and finally look at each other)*

WYKOWSKI . . . Okay, what are we going to do about this?

EUGENE Don't say it, Wykowski. Just don't say it.

WYKOWSKI I don't have to say it. We all know who he's talking about. We all know who it is. You even wrote it down in your book, didn't you? . . . Well, didn't you?

EUGENE I also wrote down you're an animal. If I'm right, then you should be in the cavalry with a saddle on your back. I'll show it to Toomey, okay? Then Epstein can start serving his five years and

77

you can move into the stables. That should satisfy a horse's ass like you.

CARNEY    Cut it out! Both of you! It's none of our business. Let the Army take care of it.

SELRIDGE    No more base privileges? No more weekend passes? You're telling me that's not my business.

HENNESEY    Carney's right. The Army'll take care of it.

EUGENE *(To EPSTEIN)*    I'm sorry, Arnold. I swear to God, I'm sorry I ever wrote it.

EPSTEIN *(Cheerfully)*    Actually I'm rather enjoying it. It's like an Agatha Christie story. *Murder by Fellatio.* Title's no good. Sounds like Italian ice cream . . . How about *Murder on the Fellatio Express?*

WYKOWSKI    You think this is funny, Epstein? Let's see if you'll be laughing at Leavenworth . . . And he calls *me* a cretin.

HENNESEY    There's nothing we can do about it tonight. Why don't we hit the sack.
    *(He gets into his bunk)*

SELRIDGE *(Getting into his bunk)*    I don't see what's such a big deal. A guy should be able to do what he wants to do . . . Just as long as he doesn't do it to me.
    *(He glares at EPSTEIN. EUGENE takes a page from his memoirs, tears it out and rips it up)*

EPSTEIN    That's a mistake, Gene . . . Once you start compromising your thoughts, you're a candidate for mediocrity.
    *(They all get into their bunks. The lights go out except a pin spot on EUGENE, who sits up and looks at the audience)*

EUGENE  . . . I learned a very important lesson that night. People believe whatever they read. Something magical happens once it's put down on paper. They figure no one would go to the trouble of writing it down if it wasn't the truth. Responsibility was my new watchword. *(We hear a phone ring once)* Anyway, the Army must have really scared Private Harvey J. Lindstrom that night because I knew when I heard the phone ring in Sergeant Toomey's room, the poor guy must have talked his guts out. I went out for a smoke because what happened in the next ten seconds was something I didn't want to see or hear.

> *(The lights in the barracks go on and* SERGEANT TOOMEY *stands there in his pants, his shirt unbuttoned and strapping a Sam Browne belt, which holds a pistol in a holster. He stands there a moment. He is not happy about the task he is about to perform. The others sit up and look at him)*

TOOMEY  When the following soldier's name is called, he is requested to dress in his class A uniform . . . and follow me . . . Hennesey, James J.!
> *(The others look surprised and turn toward* HENNESEY*)*

HENNESEY  . . . What for?

TOOMEY  That's a matter you can discuss with the military police . . . Come on, son. I don't like this any better than you do.
> *(* HENNESEY *looks at the others for help. There is none forthcoming. He gets up and slips into his pants. He puts on his shirt and begins to button it. He steps down front, away from the group, putting his tie on. He suddenly begins to sob.*

*Lights out on the barracks.*
*Light up on* EUGENE *in limbo)*

EUGENE *(To the audience)* . . . I felt real lousy about
Hennesey . . . The next weekend I went to Rowena's
again . . . She didn't even remember me . . . She acted
like I was a stranger . . . I tell her about Hennesey
doing it with another guy and maybe getting five
years in jail and she says, "Well, I haven't got too
much sympathy for their kind, sweetheart. They're
just taking the bread out of the mouths of my ba-
bies" . . . I'm never going to pay for it again . . . It
just cheapens the whole idea of sex . . . *(The sets begin
to change into the U.S.O.)* . . . I was determined to meet
the perfect girl. I knew just what she would be like
. . . She's going to be pretty but not too beautiful.
When they're too beautiful, they love them first and
you second . . . And she'll be athletic. Someone I
could hit fly balls to and she'd catch all of them.
She'll love to go to the movies and read books and
see plays and we'd never run out of conversation
. . . She's out there, I know it. Right now the girl I'm
going to fall in love with is living in New York or
Boston or Philadelphia—walking around the
streets, not even knowing I'm alive. It's crazy.
*(Lights up on U.S.O.* DAISY *is dancing with a soldier)*
There she is and here I am. The both of us just
waiting around to meet. Why doesn't she just yell
out, "Eugene! I'm here! Come and get me" . . .
*(The dance ends. The soldier goes off.* DAISY *walks
over to* EUGENE)

DAISY  Hello.

EUGENE *(Turns)* Hi.
*(He looks to the audience, then back to* DAISY)

DAISY  Would you care to dance?

EUGENE  Me? Oh. Well, I don't dance very well.

DAISY  I bet you do.

EUGENE  No. I swear. I never dance.

DAISY  Then why did you come to a dance?

EUGENE  That's a logical question. Because I like to talk. And I was hoping I'd meet someone I felt like talking to.

DAISY  We could talk while we dance.

EUGENE  It's hard for me because I'm always counting when I dance. Whatever you said, I would answer, "one two, one two."

DAISY  (*Laughs*)  Well, I'll only ask you mathematical questions. (EUGENE *laughs as well*) I'll bet you didn't know how to march before you got into the army.

EUGENE  No, I didn't.

DAISY  Well, if you could learn to march, you can learn to dance.

EUGENE  Yeah, except if I didn't learn to march, I'd be doing push-ups till I was eighty-three.

DAISY  I'm not that strict. But if it makes you that uncomfortable I won't intrude on your privacy. It was very nice meeting you. Goodbye.
    (*She starts to walk away. She gets a few steps when* EUGENE *calls out*)

EUGENE  Okay!

DAISY  Okay what?

EUGENE  One two, one two.

DAISY  Are you sure?

EUGENE   Positive.

DAISY   Good.
*(She walks over to him, then stands in front of him
and raises her left arm up and right arm in position
to hold his wrist)*

EUGENE   All I have to do is step into place, right?

DAISY   Right. *(He tucks his cap in his belt and then steps
into place, taking her hand and her waist and he starts to
dance. It's not Fred Astaire but it's not too awkward)*
You're doing fine. Except your lips are moving.

EUGENE   If my lips don't move, my feet don't move.

DAISY   Well, try talking instead of counting.

EUGENE   Okay . . . Let's see . . . My name is Gene.
*(Softly)* One two, one two . . . Sorry.

DAISY   It's okay. We're making headway. Just plain
Gene?

EUGENE   If you want the long version, it's Eugene
Morris Jerome. What's yours?

DAISY   Daisy!

EUGENE   Daisy? That's funny because Daisy's my favorite character in literature.

DAISY   Daisy Miller or Daisy Buchanan?

EUGENE   Buchanan. *The Great Gatsby* is one of the all-
time great books. Actually I never read *Daisy Miller*.
Is it good?

DAISY   It's wonderful. Although I preferred *The Great
Gatsby*. New York must have been thrilling in the
twenties.

EUGENE   It was, it was . . . That's where I'm from
. . . Well, I only saw a little of it from my baby
carriage, but it's still a terrific city . . . What else?

DAISY  What else what?

EUGENE  What other books have you read? I mean, you don't just read books with Daisy in the title, do you?

DAISY  No. I like books with Anna in the title too. *Anna Karenina . . . Anna Christie.* That was a play by O'Neill.

EUGENE  *Eugene* O'Neill. Playwrights named Eugene are usually my favorite . . . Listen, can we sit down? I've stepped on your toes three times so far and you haven't said a word. You deserve a rest. *(They sit)* I can't believe I'm having a conversation like this in Biloxi, Mississippi.

DAISY  You don't like Biloxi?

EUGENE  Oh, it's not a bad town. It's all right . . . it's okay . . . I hate it!

DAISY  I'm not that fond of it myself. Actually I'm from Gulfport. We all are.

EUGENE  Gulfport? No kidding? I know a girl from Gulfport.

DAISY  Really? Who is she? Maybe I know her.

EUGENE  Oh no . . . I doubt it. She's in the clothing business . . . Do you go to school there?

DAISY *(Nods)*  Mm hmm. St. Mary's. It's Catholic. An all girls' school. I really have to move on. We're supposed to mingle. If we're with anyone more than ten minutes, the Sisters get very nervous.

EUGENE  We haven't used up ten minutes yet . . . Please! I really like talking to you.

DAISY  Well . . . just a few minutes.

EUGENE  Would you like a Coke or something?

DAISY  It's way on the other side of the room. You could use up at least a minute and a half getting it.

EUGENE  You're right. Let the next guy get you a Coke . . . Listen, I know this is going to sound a little prejudiced, but I didn't think there were any girls in the South like you . . . I mean so easy to talk to.

DAISY  Oh, there are, believe me. Anyway, I'm not really from the South. I was raised in Chicago. My father used to work on a newspaper there. Then he got a job in New Orleans on the *Examiner* as City Editor, but he took six months off first to write a book.

EUGENE  Your father's a writer? That's incredible because that's what I want to be. Listen, not to get off the subject, but would it offend you very much if I told you that I thought you were extremely pretty?

DAISY  No. Why should it? I like it when boys think I'm pretty.

EUGENE  Do lots of boys think you're pretty?

DAISY  I hope so but they don't always say it. They get very shy around me. My dad thinks I intimidate boys my own age. I'm glad you don't seem intimidated.

EUGENE  Well, no. I told you, I'm from New York.

DAISY  . . . What kind of writer do you want to be?

EUGENE  I don't know yet. So far all I've written is a few short stories and my memoirs. I keep a notebook and write down all my thoughts and what I feel about things. I've been doing it since I was a kid.

DAISY  My father kept a journal the last few years too. That's how he got to write this book. I read that that was a very good way to become a writer.

EUGENE  Well, a few people read my memoirs and they were very impressed.

DAISY  . . . Sister Marissa is glaring at me across the room, so I'd better see if someone else wants to dance. *(She gets up)* I had a very nice time talking to you, Eugene Morris Jerome. I'm trying to remember your whole name in case I ever see it in print someday.

EUGENE  You didn't tell me your whole name in case I ever wanted to write a letter to St. Mary's Catholic All Girl School in Gulfport.

DAISY  Hannigan. Daisy Hannigan.

EUGENE  Daisy Hannigan. Great name. F. Scott Fitzgerald should have thought of that before Buchanan.

DAISY  Well, you have my permission to use it. I wouldn't mind at all being immortalized. *(She extends her hand)* Goodbye, Eugene.

EUGENE  Goodbye, Daisy . . . God, every time I say that name I feel like I'm speaking literature.

DAISY  You say nice things. As a matter of fact, you didn't say one wrong thing in that entire conversation . . . Goodbye.

*(She goes.* EUGENE *watches after her, then turns to the audience)*

EUGENE  At last, something to live for! . . . Daisy Hannigan! . . . Just try saying that name to yourself and see if you don't fall in love . . . I knew I had to see

85

her again. When she smiled at me, I had tiny little heart attacks. Not enough to kill you, but just enough to keep you from walking straight. Daisy Hannigan! Daisy Hannigan!

(*He dances off alone, Astaire-like.*

*Lights up on* TOOMEY's *room.* EPSTEIN *sits on the stool quietly looking at* TOOMEY, *who sits on the bed.* TOOMEY *takes a long swig from the bourbon bottle. He is clearly smashed*)

TOOMEY   Have a drink.

EPSTEIN   I don't drink.

TOOMEY   You will tonight.

EPSTEIN   Why?

TOOMEY (*Pulls a .45 pistol and points it*)   Because I say so.

EPSTEIN (*Drinks, sputters*)   Fine!

TOOMEY   You hate the Army, don't you, Epstein?

EPSTEIN   Yes, Sergeant, I do.

TOOMEY   Well, I don't blame you. The Army hates you just as much. When they picked you, they picked the bottom of the dung heap. You are *dung*, Epstein!... You don't mind my saying that, do you? Because you know that's what you are. Ding dong *dung!*

EPSTEIN   If you say so.

TOOMEY   Damn right I say so ... I say so because I have a loaded .45 pistol in my hand ... And I am also piss-drunk. If a piss-drunk sergeant has a loaded .45 pointed at the head of a piece of dung that the piss-drunk sergeant hates and despises, how would you describe the situation, Epstein?

EPSTEIN   Delicate . . . extremely delicate.

TOOMEY   I would describe it as "fraught with the pos-
sibility of crapping in your pants." *(He laughs and
drinks)* I'll be honest with you, Epstein. I have in-
vited you into my private quarters tonight with
every intention of putting this pistol to your ear and
blowing a tunnel clear through your head.

EPSTEIN   I'm sorry to hear that.

TOOMEY   I'll bet you are . . . If I were you, I'd consider
that "bad news from home" . . . *(He leans in closer,
meaner)* How's the contest going now, Epstein? I'll
bet your ass you're sorry you ever took me on, ain't
you?

EPSTEIN   Some days are not as good as others, I admit.

TOOMEY   When you attack a man, never attack his
strong points. And my strong point is Discipline. I
was weaned on Discipline. I sucked Discipline from
my mother's breast and I received it on my bare butt
at the age of five from the buckle of my father's Sam
Browne army belt . . . And I loved that bastard for
it . . . because he made me strong. Damn right
. . . He made me a leader of men. And he made me
despise the weakness in myself, the weakness that
can destroy a man's purpose in life. And the purpose of my life, Epstein, is Victory. Moral victory,
spiritual victory, victory over temptation, victory
on the battlefield and victory in a goddamn army
barracks in Biloxi, Mississippi . . . That's what my
daddy taught me, Epstein. What in hell did your
daddy teach you?

EPSTEIN   Not much . . . Two things maybe . . . Dignity
and Compassion.

TOOMEY *(Incredulously)* Dignity and Compassion???
. . . Are you shittin' me, Epstein?

EPSTEIN A piece of dung would never shit a piss-drunk sergeant with a loaded .45.

TOOMEY *(Puts the gun to* EPSTEIN's *head)* Don't test me, Epstein. I'll bury you with dignity but not much compassion . . . Why the hell do you always take me on, boy? . . . I'll outsmart you, outrank you and outlast you, you know that.

EPSTEIN I know that, Sergeant.

TOOMEY Do you know what the irony of this situation is, Epstein? Is it Epst*een* or Epst*ine*?

EPSTEIN Either one.

TOOMEY The irony is, Epsteen or Epstine, that despite the fact that you hate every disciplined bone in my body, you're gonna miss me when I go . . . Miss me like a baby misses her momma's nipple.

EPSTEIN Are you going somewhere, Sergeant?

TOOMEY Didn't I just say that? Didn't I just tell you I was leaving this base?

EPSTEIN No, Sergeant, you didn't. When are you leaving?

TOOMEY At oh seven hundred, April 3, 1943 . . . That's tomorrow morning . . . I know how much you boys are going to miss me. But I don't want anyone making a fuss or anything. No gifts, you understand. If you like, you can clean a couple of latrines for me, but that's about it.

EPSTEIN Where are you going?

TOOMEY I am reporting to Dickerson Veterans Hospital, Camp Rawlings, Roanoke, Virginia . . . I believe, in gratitude, the Army is going to replace my steel plate with sterling silver . . . That means I'll be able to hock my head in any pawn shop in this country, how 'bout that?

EPSTEIN   How long will you be gone, Sergeant?

TOOMEY   I just told you, you dumb son of a bitch. I'm going to the Veterans Hospital. They don't send you back from a Veterans Hospital. You become a Veteran. You walk around in a blue bathrobe and at night you listen to Jack Benny and play checkers with the other basket weavers . . . What I'm trying to tell you, you toilet bowl cleanser, is that my active career in the U.S. Army has been terminated.

EPSTEIN   I'm sorry to hear that, Sergeant.

TOOMEY   *(Holds up the gun again)*   Don't give me none of your goddamn compassion, Epstein . . . Compassion is just going to buy you a Star of David at the Arlington Cemetery.

EPSTEIN   Yes, Sergeant.

TOOMEY   They can put sixty-five pounds of nuts and bolts in my head, give me a brown tweed suit and a job pumping gas, I will still be the best damned top sergeant you'll ever meet in your short but sweet life, Epsteen-or-Epstine.

EPSTEIN   I'm sure of that, Sergeant.

TOOMEY   One night from my room here, I heard a game being played in the barracks. I heard Jerome ask each and every man what they would want if they had one last week to live . . . I played the game right along with you and put my five bucks down on my bunk just like the rest of you. *(He takes out a bill*) Here's my money. You tell me if I would have won the game.

EPSTEIN  The game is over, Sergeant.

TOOMEY  Not yet, boy. Not yet . . . All right. You know what I would do with my last week on earth?

EPSTEIN  What's that, Sergeant?

TOOMEY  I would like to take one army rookie, the greatest misfit dumb-ass malcontent sub-human useless son of a bitch I ever came across and turn him into an obedient, disciplined soldier that this army could be proud of. That would be my victory. *You* are that subhuman misfit, Epstein, and by God, before I leave here, I'm gonna do it and pick up my five dollars, you hear me?

EPSTEIN  None of us actually did it, Sergeant. It was just a game.

TOOMEY  Not to me, soldier. On your feet, Epstein!!

EPSTEIN  Really, Sergeant, I don't think you're in any condition to—

TOOMEY  ON YOUR FEET! (EPSTEIN *stands*) AT-TEN-SHUN!! (*He snaps to attention*) . . . A crime has been committed in this room tonight, Epstein. A breach of army regulations. A noncommissioned officer has threatened the life of an enlisted man, brandishing a loaded weapon at him without cause or provocation, the said act being provoked by an inebriated platoon leader while on duty . . . I am that platoon leader, Epstein, and it is your unquestioned duty to report this incident to the proper authorities.

EPSTEIN  Look, that's really not necessary, Sergean—

TOOMEY    As I am piss-drunk and dangerous, Epstein, it is also your duty to relieve me of my loaded weapon.

EPSTEIN    I never really thought you were going to shoot me, Ser—

TOOMEY    TAKE MY WEAPON, GODDAMN IT!

EPSTEIN    What do you mean, take it? How am I going to take it?

TOOMEY    *Demand* it, you weasel bastard, or I'll blow your puny brains out.

EPSTEIN    *(Calming him)* Okay, okay . . . May I have your gun, Sergeant?

TOOMEY    *Pistol,* turd head!

EPSTEIN    May I have your pistol, Sergeant?

TOOMEY    Force it out of my hand.

EPSTEIN    Force it out of your hand?

TOOMEY    Grab my wrist! If you dare! (EPSTEIN *leaps for* TOOMEY's *wrist, wrestling for the .45.* TOOMEY *finally allows him to wrest it from him)* Good!

EPSTEIN    Okay. Thanks. Now why don't you just try to get a good night's sleep and—

TOOMEY    To properly charge me, you'll need witnesses . . . Call in the platoon.

EPSTEIN    The platoon? You don't want to do that in front of all—

TOOMEY    CALL THEM IN, SOLDIER!!

EPSTEIN    *(Sighs, walks to the door and opens it)* Hey, guys. You want to come in here a minute. (EPSTEIN *comes back in. To* TOOMEY) This is not going to change

91

anything between us, Sergeant. This is just as illogical and insane as before.

TOOMEY   Maybe. But it's regulations. And as long as you obey regulations, Epstein, I win. (WYKOWSKI, SELRIDGE, CARNEY *and* EUGENE *enter the room in various states of undress.* EUGENE *is in his Class A's. They all seem confused*) Men . . . as you can see, I'm pissed to the gills and have just threatened to blow Epstein's brains out . . . Private Epstein has relieved me of my weapon and placed me under arrest. You are all witnesses. (*They look at each other*) Private Epstein will now take his prisoner to Company headquarters to file charges and complaints . . . I would just like to add that Private Epstein has displayed outstanding courage and has carried out his duty in the manner of a first-rate soldier. I am putting him up for commendation. (*He smiles at* EPSTEIN *triumphantly*) I'm ready when you are, soldier . . . We're wasting time, Epstein. Let's go.

EPSTEIN   I'm not going to do it. I'm not going to file charges!

TOOMEY   Remember what your father taught you, Epstein . . . Show some to a man who's going to Virginia tomorrow.

EPSTEIN (*Looking at* TOOMEY)   . . . Suppose you just get company punishment like the rest of us?

TOOMEY   You can handle this any way you want. As long as justice is served.
   (*They all look at* EPSTEIN)

EPSTEIN   . . . Sergeant Toomey! . . .

TOOMEY   Ho!

EPSTEIN  I'll drop all charges and complaints if you give me two hundred push-ups.

TOOMEY  I accept your compassionate offer, Epstein.

EPSTEIN  Thank you. On the floor—please. (TOOMEY *drops*) Count off!!

TOOMEY  Yes, Private Epstein. (*He starts push-ups, first slowly, then rapidly*) One . . . two . . . three . . . four . . . five . . . six . . . seven . . . eight . . .

SELRIDGE  I don't freakin' believe this.

TOOMEY  —nine—ten—eleven—twelve—
(*The lights fade on* TOOMEY'*s room as he continues push-ups.* EUGENE *steps down front*)

EUGENE  Epstein won the fantasy game fair and square because *his* really came true . . . In a way they both won because if for only one brief moment, Toomey had turned Arnold into the best soldier in the platoon . . . The next day Toomey went to the Veterans Hospital in Virginia and we never saw him again . . . Our new sergeant was sane, logical and a decent man, and after four weeks with him, we realized how much we missed Sergeant Toomey . . . One should never underestimate the stimulation of eccentricity . . . Daisy and I corresponded three times a week and I visited her twice in Gulfport and the most we ever did was hold hands. I was either too shy or she was too Catholic . . . Finally we finished basic training and I knew we'd be shipping out soon. (DAISY *appears, carrying a small wrapped package.* EUGENE *smiles when she appears*) Hi.

DAISY  Hello.
(*They reach out and hold each other's hand*)

93

EUGENE  Your hand feels cold.

DAISY  Yours feels warm.

EUGENE  Would you like to go somewhere? Down by the lake? Or to Overton's Hotel. They have dancing till midnight . . . Or we could just walk.

DAISY  I can't. I've got to be back in ten minutes. I shouldn't even be out now.

EUGENE  *Ten minutes???* . . . Are you serious? I came all the way from Biloxi.

DAISY  I know. But it's Good Friday.

EUGENE  Isn't that a holiday?

DAISY  No. It's a Holy Day. It's the day that Christ our Lord died. We have to abstain from parties or movies or dates. It's a day of prayer and mourning.

EUGENE  So why do they call it Good Friday? It sounds like Lousy Friday to me. Ten minutes, Jesus! Sorry, no Jesus. I can't believe it.

DAISY  It's my fault. I should have told you in my last letter . . . We can make up for it next week, can't we?

EUGENE  I'm not sure I'll be here next Friday. We finished basic training yesterday. We could be shipping out any day now.

DAISY  Shipping out? To where?

EUGENE  Europe. The Pacific. They haven't told us yet.

DAISY  Overseas? So soon?

EUGENE  Well, they can't keep us here forever. The army needs reinforcements. We've already lost a private and a sergeant and we're still in Biloxi

. . . Can't you stay out a little later? Just tonight? I know I'm Jewish but I don't think Christ your Lord is going to hold it against you personally.

DAISY  I can't, Eugene. I have to be faithful to my beliefs.

EUGENE  What about being faithful to me?

DAISY  I have been. I haven't been to another U.S.O. dance since we met. I just don't feel like dancing with anyone else anymore.

EUGENE  Do you mean that?

DAISY  Cross my heart.
(She's about to)

EUGENE  Don't cross it. Religion is always getting in our way. I believe you.

DAISY  I think you're a very special person, Eugene. If you want me to, I'll write to you as often as you want.

EUGENE  Of course I do. I want you to write me every day. And I want a picture. I don't even have a picture of you.

DAISY  What kind of picture?

EUGENE  Do you have one where I could feel your skin?

DAISY  If I did, I wish I had one where I could squeeze your hand.

EUGENE  . . . I'm going to shoot my foot, I swear. I don't want to leave here.

DAISY  I'm glad you feel the same way about me, Eugene.

EUGENE  You know I do . . . I'd have come tonight even if I knew I only had *five* minutes with you . . . Daisy, I—I—

DAISY  What, Eugene?

EUGENE  I want to say something but I'm having a lot of trouble with the words.

DAISY  That doesn't sound like Eugene the Writer to me.

EUGENE  Well, I'm not writing now. I'm Eugene the Talker . . . Daisy, I just want to tell you I—I— goddamn it, why can't I say it? . . . Oooh! I'm sorry. I apologize. I didn't mean to say that. Especially on Good Friday.

DAISY  I'll say ten Hail Mary's for you.

EUGENE  You don't have to do that. They're not going to do *me* any good.

DAISY  What is it you wanted to say?

EUGENE  Ah, Daisy, you know what it is. I've never said it to a girl in my life. I don't know what it's going to sound like when it comes out.

DAISY  Say it and I'll tell you.

EUGENE  *(Takes a deep breath)*  . . . I love you, Daisy. *(He exhales)* Ah, nuts. It came out wrong. It's not the way I meant it.

DAISY  I've never heard it said so beautifully.

EUGENE  What do you mean? How many other guys have said it to you?

DAISY  None. I meant in the movies. Not Tyrone Power or Robert Taylor or even Clark Gable.

EUGENE   Yeah, well, they get paid for saying it. I'm in business for myself.

DAISY *(Laughs)*   I remember everything you say to me. When I go home at night, I write them all down and I read them over whenever I miss you.

EUGENE   Well, if you're writing your memoirs, keep your locker closed. I don't want to be the talk of St. Mary's.
*(We hear church bells chime)*

DAISY   It's eight o'clock. I've got to go.

EUGENE   You didn't say it to me yet.

DAISY   That I love you?

EUGENE   No. Not like that. You threw it in too quickly . . . You have to take a breath, prepare for it and then say it.

DAISY   All right. *(She inhales)* I've taken a breath . . . *(She waits)* Now I'm preparing for it . . . And now I'll say it . . . I love you, Eugene. *(He moves to kiss her)* We can't kiss. It's Good Friday.

EUGENE   You *have* to kiss after you say "I love you." Not even God would forgive you that.

DAISY   All right . . . I love you, Eugene. *(She kisses him lightly on the lips)* I have to go.

EUGENE   Daisy! This is the most important moment of our lives. It's the first time we're in love. That only happens once . . . When I leave tonight, I don't know if we'll ever see each other again.

DAISY   Don't say that, Eugene. Please don't say that.

EUGENE   It's possible. I pray it doesn't happen, but it's possible . . . I need a proper kiss, Daisy. A kiss to

97

commemorate a night I'll never forget as long as I live. *(She looks at him)* I'll even say a hundred Hail Mary's for you on the bus ride back . . . Okay?
*(She smiles and nods. He takes her in his arms and kisses her warmly and passionately . . . When they part, she seems weak)*

DAISY   I think you'd better say two hundred on the bus . . . Oh. I almost forgot. This is for you. It's a book.

EUGENE   Really? What book? I love your taste in books.

DAISY   It's blank pages. For your memoirs. Page one can start with tonight. *(She hugs* EUGENE*)* Take care of yourself, Eugene Morris Jerome . . . Even if some other girls gets you, I'll always know I was your first love.
*(She runs off)*

EUGENE   I knew at that moment I was a long way from becoming a writer because there were no words I could find to describe the happiness I felt in those ten minutes with Daisy Hannigan.
*(Lights up on the coach train seen at the opening of the play. It is night and the train rattles by in the semidarkness. The same group as we saw in the first scene are in their Class A's, stretched out on the coach seats.* WYKOWSKI, SELRIDGE *and* CARNEY *are all asleep.* EUGENE *is writing in his new book of memoirs.* EPSTEIN, *once again, is sleeping in the rack above them . . .* ROY'S *shoeless foot is practically in* WYKOWSKI'S *mouth.* WYKOWSKI *slaps it away)*

WYKOWSKI   Jesus, change your socks, will you? What is that, a new secret weapon?

SELRIDGE  I *did* change them. This one used to be on the other foot.
(*He giggles*)

CARNEY  You creeps never grow up. I'll tell you one thing. After the war, I'm not having any reunions with you guys.

EUGENE  Hey, Arnold! How do you spell "vicissitude"?

EPSTEIN  You don't! Leave it out. Try for simplicity. The critics will use vicissitude in their reviews.

CARNEY  Did you guys hear about Hennesey?

SELRIDGE  What?

CARNEY  He only got three months in the can. That's not so bad. After that, he's out of this war.

WYKOWSKI  With a dishonorable discharge? He better pray we lose because no one in *this* country's gonna give him a job.

SELRIDGE  The army's nuts. They shouldn't let guys like that out. They should keep them together in one outfit. "The Fruit Brigade" . . . Make them nurses or something.

EPSTEIN  You hear that, Eugene? We are listening to the generation that will inherit America. It's inevitable that one of these geniuses will someday be President of the United States.

WYKOWSKI  Listen to him, will ya? Thinks he's real tough 'cause he took Toomey's gun away. We'll see how tough he is when he hits the beach.

EPSTEIN  I have to warn you, Kowski, that I expect to be very seasick on the troopship. And wherever you sleep, I'm going to be in the hammock above you.

CARNEY How about getting some sleep *now?* This may be the best bed we see for a few *years.*
*(It turns silent as the train rumbles on.*
EUGENE *has been writing in his memoirs. He turns to the audience)*

EUGENE So far, two of my main objectives came true . . . I lost my virginity and I fell in love. Now all I had to do was become a writer and stay alive . . . On that first train ride to Biloxi, we were all nervous . . . On the train now heading for an Atlantic seaport, we were all scared . . . I closed my notebook and tried to sleep . . . *(He closes the notebook)* When I opened the notebook two years later, I was on a train just like this one, heading for Fort Dix, New Jersey, to be discharged . . . I reread what I wrote to see how accurate my predictions were the night Wykowski broke into my locker . . . Roy Selridge served in every campaign in France, was eventually made a sergeant and sent back to Biloxi to train new recruits. He has men doing three hundred push-ups a day . . . Wykowski was wounded at Arnheim by a mortar shell. He lost his right leg straight up to the hip. He didn't get the Medal of Honor, but he was cited for outstanding courage in battle . . . Don Carney, after six months of constant attack by enemy fire, was hospitalized for severe depression and neurological disorders. He never sings any more . . . Arnold Epstein was listed as missing in action and his body was never traced or found. But Arnold's a tricky guy. He might still be alive teaching philosophy in Greece somewhere. He just never liked doing things the army way . . . Daisy Hannigan married a doctor from New Orleans. Her name is now Daisy Horowitz. Oh, well . . . She sends me a postcard every time she has a new baby . . . As for me, I never saw a day's action. I was in a jeep accident my first day in England and my back was so badly injured, they wanted to send me home. Instead they gave me a job writing for *Stars and Stripes*, the G.I. newspaper. I still suffer pangs of guilt because my career was enhanced by World War II . . . I'll tell you one thing, I'm glad I didn't know all that the night our train left Biloxi for places and events unknown!

CARNEY *(Singing)*
    Tangerine, you are all they claim
    With your eyes of night
    And lips as bright as flame
    Tangerine, when she passes by
    Señoritas stare
    And caballeros sigh . . .
            *Curtain*

Since 1960, a Broadway season without a Neil Simon comedy or musical has been a rare one. His first play was *Come Blow Your Horn*, followed by the musical *Little Me*. During the 1966–67 season, *Barefoot in the Park*, *The Odd Couple*, *Sweet Charity* and *The Star-Spangled Girl* were all running simultaneously; in the 1970–71 season, Broadway theatergoers had their choice of *Plaza Suite*, *Last of the Red Hot Lovers* and *Promises, Promises*. Next came *The Gingerbread Lady*, *The Prisoner of Second Avenue*, *The Sunshine Boys*, *The Good Doctor*, *God's Favorite*, *California Suite*, *Chapter Two*, *They're Playing Our Song*, *I Ought to Be in Pictures*, *Fools*, a revival of *Little Me*, *Brighton Beach Memoirs*, *Biloxi Blues* (which won the Tony Award for "Best Play"), the female version of *The Odd Couple* and the forthcoming *Broadway Bound*.

NEIL SIMON began his writing career in television, writing *The Phil Silvers Show* and Sid Caesar's *Your Show of Shows*. Mr. Simon has also written for the screen: the adaptations of *Barefoot in the Park*, *The Odd Couple*, *Plaza Suite*, *The Prisoner of Second Avenue*, *The Sunshine Boys*, *California Suite*, *Chapter Two*, *I Ought to Be in Pictures* and the forthcoming *Brighton Beach Memoirs*. His other screenplays include *The Out-of-Towners*, *The Heartbreak Kid*, *Murder by Death*, *The Goodbye Girl*, *The Cheap Detective*, *Seems Like Old Times*, *Only When I Laugh*, *Max Dugan Returns* and *The Slugger's Wife*.

The author lives in California and New York. He has two daughters, Ellen and Nancy.